LABOURING FOR PEACE

A history of the campaign inside the Labour Party
for international peace

Grace Crookall-Greening and Rosalie Huzzard

Published in 2011 by CAM Yorkshire
58 Ward Street, Penistone S36 6EP
www.camyorkshire.wordpress.com

Printed by Beamreach
22 Pepper Street, Lymm, Cheshire WA13 0JB
www.beamreachuk.co.uk

ISBN 978-0- 9532423-6-8

Front cover photograph:
Anti Gulf War March, Hyde Park, London, February 2nd 1991
(Rosalie Huzzard)

ACKNOWLEDGEMENTS

We thank the following for their contributions to this publication: Tony Benn, Tam Dalyell, Beryl Huffinley, Jim Mortimer and Stan Newens. We thank Patricia Daniel for her encouragement, expert advice and editorial skill. We are also grateful for the legacies received from Frank Allaun and Lord Hugh Jenkins and the Ron Huzzard Memorial Fund, without which this book could not have been funded.

The photograph of Frank Allaun on page 2 is from *Frank Allaun: A tribute by Hyman Davies,* The Working Class Movement Library, 2003 (page 3), reproduced with kind permission of WCML; the poster "And Now - Win the Peace – Vote Labour" (1945-1948) on page 11 is reproduced with kind permission of The Museum of London; the photograph of George Lansbury on page 13 is reproduced courtesy of Wikimedia Creative Commons Copyright; the photograph of the early Aldermaston March on page 35 is reproduced courtesy of the CND Archive; and the photograph of The Greenham Marcher on page 61 is reproduced by kind permission of Thalia Campbell.

ABOUT THE AUTHORS

Grace Crookall-Greening joined the Labour Action for Peace executive committee in 1999 and edited its publications from then until 2006, during which time she served as Chair for one year. She also worked as editor and media secretary in the Quaker international department (Quaker Peace and Service) and admired her colleague Ron Huzzard's dedicated work for peace, disarmament and socialism. Leaving school at 14, she first worked in a Manchester newspaper office and benefited later from Labour's great gift to the 1970s and the future: The Open University. From her father, a Royal Army Medical Corps stretcher bearer in France and Gallipoli in the First World War, she inherited the dilemma of pacifism versus military action. She is optimistic enough to believe that humanity could evolve beyond war and replace military forces by an international security and development service, which would intervene to protect potential war victims before it is too late.

Rosalie Huzzard has been a member of the Labour Party since 1951. She has held most posts at borough, constituency and branch level. She was a full time Secretary Organiser for two Constituency Labour Parties in the 1970s and has run many election campaigns in the London Borough of Bromley. She was political secretary to the Greater London Council and Inner London Education Authority Labour Groups in the early 1980s when Ken Livingstone was Leader of the GLC. She now lives in Sheffield in the Heeley constituency. Inspired by her husband's work, she has been active in the peace movement since the 1950s, as a Quaker, through the Campaign for Nuclear Disarmament, Labour Action for Peace and other groups. A former President of the UK section of the Women's International League for Peace and Freedom (WILPF), she has been active internationally, nationally and locally. Her main focus now is on sustainable development, which she sees as inter-related to peace, social justice and human rights.

*We hope this book will inspire younger socialists
in the Labour and trade union movements to work for
progressive policies, so that Britain leads the way in
ensuring a peaceful world built on social justice for all
and a sustainable future.*

CONTENTS

FOREWORD

This history of Labour Action for Peace is a must for the growing number of people opposed to the wars waged by Britain and America since the Second World War. It also shows what can be done by committed people in an organisation that does not want to be disturbed by radical thoughts - the Labour Party - which seemed stuck with the ideas that were pumped out by the defence departments and the media denouncing those who argue that there is an alternative to war.

Reading the book reminds me of the whole political history of over sixty years, from the Hiroshima bomb to the Afghan war and Iraq, including Suez, Vietnam, the Falklands and the Israeli attack on Gaza. Throughout the period people such as Fenner Brockway, Frank Cousins, Frank Allaun and many from CND including Ron Huzzard, Walter Wolfgang and Jeremy Corbyn (to name a few) were forever attempting to find peace, on trips abroad and on delegations arguing the case for disarmament and particularly nuclear disarmament.

The clear resolutions that were prepared and presented to the Labour Party Conference or the National Executive in the hope of changing party policy were always in hand and did have a role in shifting party policy albeit very slowly.

This is the story of campaigning, and always has been, when determined people at the bottom start making demands for justice from the people at the top. This should be the inspiration for our work at the next election, putting forward demands for nuclear disarmament, human rights and peace and justice here and worldwide. Labour Action for Peace has a central role in Labour history that we should never forget and which should inspire us to do what has to be done.

Tony Benn

1

TRIBUTES

Labouring for Peace is published as a tribute to the two people who perhaps did more than anyone to bring peace and disarmament issues to the forefront of Labour Party policy:
Frank Allaun and Ron Huzzard.

A Tribute to Frank Allaun
By Stan Newens
(Former MP for Epping and then Harlow, MEP for London, Labour historian and former Vice Chair, Labour Action for Peace)

Frank Allaun

Frank Allaun, who died in November 2002 aged 89, was a dedicated campaigner for peace and left causes, who never deviated or gave up. His refusal to compromise cost him all hope of Government office but he contributed much more to the Labour cause as a champion of the Party and fundamental ideas.

Born to Jewish parents Harry and Harriet Allaun, he was educated at Manchester Grammar School and night school, but his reading gave him a profound hatred of war. In 1932 he became secretary of

Manchester Anti-War Council and joined the Communist Party, being elected in due course to the Manchester District Committee. In the 1930s he also became secretary of the Manchester Left Book Club, a WEA tutor and organised trips abroad.

His ambition was to become a journalist and during the course of the Second World War, while he worked at Vickers Armstrong as an engineer, he edited the *Vickers Factory News*. In 1945 he became a full-time reporter, later industrial correspondent for the *Manchester Evening News*. Subsequently he became Northern Industrial Correspondent for the *Daily Herald*. In his own leisure time from 1951 to 1967 he edited *Labour's Northern Voice,* publishing 16 editions and 50,000 copies.

By 1944 he had become disillusioned with the Communist Party and was deeply offended by the article in the *Daily Worker* by the Soviet novelist Ilya Ehrenburg, suggesting that all Germans were Nazis. He therefore left and joined the Labour Party. In 1955 he was elected as Labour MP for Salford East. Apart from working hard for his constituents, Frank concentrated his activities on peace and housing. In 1956 he opposed the Eden Government's Suez operation. In 1957 he wrote a pamphlet, *Stop the H-Bomb Race*. In 1958 he helped organise the first Aldermaston march, following the formation of the Campaign for Nuclear Disarmament. His objective was to win the Party over to unilateral nuclear disarmament, which was formally achieved at the 1960 Labour Party Annual Conference. Thereafter he was one who tried to resist Hugh Gaitskell's successful bid to reverse the decision the following year.

When Labour won the 1964 general election under a new leader, Harold Wilson, Frank became Parliamentary Private Secretary to Tony Greenwood, Colonial Secretary, but he resigned after 5 months to speak out against American armed intervention in Vietnam. As a member of the newly formed Tribune Group of MPs, he was one of a handful who stood firm for an abstention in a Commons vote in July 1966, to demonstrate opposition to the American bombing campaign. Thirty five MPs eventually took part, firmly re-establishing an anti-war position in the Labour Party.

In the chair of the Labour Peace Fellowship, later Labour Action for Peace, Frank led an active group of rank and filers, while he spoke and abstained with others in the House of Commons on votes to increase arms expenditure, to promote the arms trade and to supply arms for doubtful causes (for example, civil war in Nigeria).

In 1967 he was elected to the National Executive Committee of the Labour Party, on which he continued to sit until 1991, chairing the Labour Party in 1979. Here, as in the House of Commons, he opposed Barbara Castle's White Paper, *In Place of Strife,* to limit trade union rights, and also disarmament and for greater party democracy.

Frank campaigned relentlessly for building homes and wrote a book *No Place like Home* on his housing policies in 1972.

After his retirement in 1983 he remained active, becoming Vice President of CND and as Chair and later President of Labour Action for Peace, attending meetings and writing pieces for the press. He brushed aside compliments, insisting that rank and file activists were never fully recognised for their contributions and that he had been lucky to hold positions which had given him great influence and the affection of many ordinary Labour Party members.

In his personal life he was abstemious and enjoyed simple pursuits like walking and swimming. He was deeply attached to his family - his first wife, Lillian Hall, who died in 1986; his son and daughter and

4

their families; and his second wife, Millie Bobker, whom he married in 1989. He had a lively personality and a good sense of humour and was a staunch friend. None were truer to the cause that he upheld for more than 70 years.

A Tribute to Ron Huzzard
By Jim Mortimer
(Former national official of the Association of Engineering and Shipbuilding Draughtsmen (AESD), former Chairman of the Advisory, Conciliation and Arbitration Service (ACAS) and former General Secretary of the Labour Party)

Ron Huzzard 1964 (RH)

The history of Labour Action for Peace is inseparable from the name of Ron Huzzard. A founder member, he had been active from the start. Apart from a few years in the 1980s he edited its newsletter from the 1940s until the 1990s. He was the Secretary from 1985 until his death in 1998. He had all the attributes of competence. He was efficient and diligent in the discharge of his secretarial duties. Personally, he was friendly and helpful, persuasive but not dogmatic. He was well informed and strongly committed to the aims of Labour Action for Peace. He was a good listener but he was not backward in

5

giving political leadership. In short, he was quite exceptional in the qualities that made him so prominent in the affairs of an organisation that combined activity for peace with a commitment to the labour movement.

I first met Ron about 63 years ago. We were both evening students at the London School of Economics on a three year course of trade union and industrial relations studies. We held awards for our studies from the Trade Union Council.

We were both members of the same union, then known as the Association of Engineering and Shipbuilding Draughtsmen. Subsequently, through a series of amalgamations, it has become part of UNITE, now Britain's largest trade union.

One of Ron's special qualities was that he never divorced his convictions about the struggle for peace from the need to mobilise support for peace activity within the labour movement - which he believed was the main vehicle through which pressure had to be exerted.

It was this conviction that made him so active both with the trade union movement and in the Labour Party. Within the union he was prominent at every level. He was a branch officer and delegate to the union's district council. He was a regular delegate to the annual conference of the union and a prominent participant in debates, not only on peace issues but also on wider trade union activities. He was always listened to with respect.

Ron played the leading role in persuading the unions' annual conference to affiliate to the National Peace Council and to the Union of Democratic Control. The NPC had international associations and I recall that on one occasion he and I attended a conference in

Germany on behalf of our union, to discuss, among other problems, the growing threat of re-armament in Europe.

Ron was not only an active trade unionist; he was also an active member of the Labour Party. He and his wife Rosalie were stalwarts of the party in Orpington, and he was a Labour councillor in the London Borough of Bromley for eighteen years, and prominent on its Education Committee.

Ron was selected for the union's parliamentary panel. Nominated candidates were interviewed at some length and were questioned about their activity in the union and in the Party and about their views on trade union and political issues. The process was rigorous, but Ron came through with the full support of the committee and his selection was endorsed by the Annual Conference. He was subsequently selected for the parliamentary seat of Croydon North West in 1955, which he did not win. He was again selected for the marginal seat of Chislehurst in 1964, where unfortunately he was narrowly defeated. Parliament thus lost an opportunity to gain a representative who would have been a great asset to his constituency, to the Labour Party and to the people of Britain.

Within his union, Ron used every legitimate means to influence opinion, in his office, his branch, his district council, at the union's annual conference and in the Labour Party. He also used the correspondence columns of the union journal.

Years later Ron was awarded the Frank Cousins Peace Award by the Transport and General Workers Union (TGWU) for his outstanding contribution to the cause of peace. It was an honour well deserved. He was a Quaker. His life was influenced by his religious views and his activity was a tribute to his beliefs. Ron's life was an example to us all.

LABOURING FOR PEACE

PROLOGUE

Strange, you may think, to start a new peace organisation in 1940, the first year of the Second World War. Not so strange, though, when you know that a strong peace culture had developed and grown in Britain in the 1920s and 1930s. The First World War had ended 22 years before, and the personal tragedies and losses were well remembered, even within the memories of quite young people

The social and political background to the years before the Second World War has a significant bearing on the story of the peace movement within the Labour Party. Some aspects of this period are discussed here as a prologue to the story of a quest lasting over 60 years.

The organisation of socialist internationalists, who opposed the war but wished to continue to work in the Labour Party, emerged as the Labour Pacifist Fellowship in 1940, with George Lansbury MP, Dr Alfred Salter MP, Reg Sorensen MP, Rhys Davies MP, Councillors Richard West, Will Elliott and Eric Messer as founder members. It became the Labour Peace Fellowship (LPF) in 1953 and Labour Action for Peace (LAP) in 1970.

Peace, socialism and disarmament were clear principles and objectives for a substantial proportion of Labour Party members from the First World War onwards. In 1940 some LPF members wanted to know how the war could be brought to a quick end. They were already too late, of course. Czechoslovakia had fallen and Hitler had occupied Poland. He had to be stopped. But how? What could pacifists and peacemakers do? At least, learn from past errors.

The Versailles Treaty had been a great concern when its content became known. Germany had signed it in 1919, but if it had not been so cruelly punitive of the German people, perhaps the "war to end all wars" would have been just that. Suppose that the defeated German nation had not been desperately short of food and other essentials in the 1920s, when their economy was wrecked by the reparations they had to make to the victors, would their better condition have made them less susceptible to fascist propaganda? Would Nazism have been able to build its power without the despair of the people?

Perhaps. But, as the nature of Nazism became apparent, perhaps not. With hindsight, people could see that if action to help had come in time, after the first war, then the second, and the terrible fate of the victims of the holocaust, just might have been prevented. After the Second World War, thank God, more wisdom and compassion prevailed.

Though the old Labour Pacifist Fellowship had changed its name, absolute pacifist members, opponents of war in all circumstances, were still amongst those most dedicated to peace.

What is the definition of a pacifist? Tony Benn, when President of Labour Action for Peace, looked it up in the *Oxford English Dictionary*. He read: "The doctrine or belief that it is desirable and possible to settle international disputes by peaceful means". That makes most sensible people pacifists. But as the word was most commonly used, it applied only to absolutists. They would probably have amended the definition to read "imperative" instead of "possible".

The Labour Party's general election campaign poster in 1945 refers to 'V for Victory' in the Second World War: and indeed the 1945 elections saw a landslide victory for the Labour Party under Clem Attlee's leadership.

11

This is what Gandhi wrote on the subject: "Whilst all violence is bad and must be condemned in the abstract, it is permissible for, and even the duty of, a believer in *ahimsa* (non-violence) to distinguish between the aggressor and the offender. Having done so he will side with the defender in a non-violent manner i.e. give his life in saving him." [1]

As citizens of Britain, we are not always asked for our consent to war, any more than the Germans were. That last great peaceful protest against the coming war in Iraq, in February 2003, did nothing to avert it, though the strength of public opinion has emerged again with the public inquiry into the war.

What then do we make of the Nuremburg Declaration? After the trial of Nazi leaders in 1946, the judges said that the German people had a responsibility to protest against the policies which caused the deaths of 6 million Jewish people and other innocent victims. At what point should the people speak out and withdraw their consent? How can that right (if it is a right) be respected?

Heated debate in Britain accompanied the rise in fascism in Spain, Italy and Germany. The civil war in Spain changed the minds of some pacifists, including Fenner Brockway, who went to Spain as a young journalist to rescue some British volunteers who were helping the Republican cause but needed to escape from the Communists. Fenner was a conscientious objector and went to prison during the First World War. He decided after his experience in Spain that a war to liberate people from oppression might sometimes be necessary.

For Christians, peacemaking has its origin in the teaching of Jesus in the New Testament. Gandhi's writing and his experience of practising non-violence was a revelation to Martin Luther King and he and his colleagues studied and practised it in the Civil Rights movement. He wrote: "It was in this Gandhian emphasis on love and non-violence that I discovered the method of social reform that I had been seeking". [2]

Peace, Disarmament and Socialism

LPF members felt, at different times, that one or all of these three ideals was ignored, neglected, or used only in rhetorical speeches by the right wing of the Party, whereas the interconnection was an essential part of the whole philosophy which had inspired many in the Party from its earliest days.

Peace
Peace between nations was never more persistently and passionately advocated than by George Lansbury[3], the pacifist Leader of the Labour Party from 1932 to 1935. "When we are asked what will become of us if we are not armed and will not fight, ask those who put this question: 'What will happen to us if we do?' Nothing that could happen could possibly be more terrible than what has happened to all those who in the past or present have put their trust in the form of murder we call war," Lansbury had written in his *Daily Herald* column as early as 1923.

George Lansbury 1938

At the 1935 Labour Party Conference, Lansbury needed to respond to the darkening international future: Japan's invasion of Manchuria, Mussolini's aggression in Abyssinia, Hitler's withdrawal from the League of Nations disarmament talks, massive German re-armament and conscription.

Lansbury had a national reputation and was a possible Prime Minister if Labour won the next election What he offered to the anxious Labour Party Conference was his plan for a world conference where the 'haves' and 'have nots' could learn about each other's needs and share economic advantages between the nations. He had called upon Baldwin, the Conservative Prime Minister, to take this initiative. In a letter to *The Times* he had suggested an inter-faith conference in Jerusalem, called by the Pope, to "bid the war spirit rest".

Though true to his own faith and long-held Christian perspective in politics, Lansbury was not seen to be seeking a programme with which his colleagues could work. He was openly anti-imperialist and wanted to break up the British Empire. In this he was twenty years too early.

Concluding his Leader's speech he said: "If mine was the only voice in this conference, I would say, in the name of the faith I hold, the belief I have is that God intended us to live peaceably and quietly with each other. If some people do not allow us to do so, I am ready to stand as the early Christians did, and say: 'This is our faith, this is where we stand, and, if necessary, this is where we will die.'"

Ernest Bevin, Leader of the Transport and General Workers Union (later to be Foreign Secretary) accused Lansbury of failing to support the policy paper, *For Peace and Socialism,* on which the vote was to

14

be taken; and attacked him for "taking your conscience around... asking to be told what to do with it."

The vote for peace was 102,000 with 2,168,000 against. Lansbury resigned his leadership. He was 76 and for the next few years he travelled the world meeting rulers to persuade them that a world conference could bring peace and restore security. He was enabled to do this by his honoured place in the peace movement as well as in the Labour Party.

A few months later, a letter appeared in the press written by a well-known clergyman, the Reverend Dick Sheppard, asking people to send him signed postcards containing the written pledge "To renounce war and never again directly or indirectly to support or sanction another." It produced a deluge of pledges at a rate of about 4,500 a day, reaching over 100,000 within weeks.

Dick Sheppard then formed the Peace Pledge Union (PPU), a membership organisation which still continues. He recruited a staff of 30 to administer it, run conferences and bring out a weekly newspaper, *Peace News*, which still continues to publish. When Dick Sheppard died, George Lansbury became PPU president.

The International Fellowship of Reconciliation, an organisation which started just before the First World War, was ready to support Lansbury and his colleague Dr Alfred Salter, MP for West Bermondsey[4] in "embassies of reconciliation". They went to the United States, where Lansbury wanted to visit President Roosevelt, in spring 1936, travelling to New York where the US Federation of Peace Societies had fixed tours for them: for George, the Eastern and Northern states (27 cities and 10 broadcasts); for Alfred, across the Mid-West to the Pacific (59 meetings, 5 broadcasts).

During his visit to President Roosevelt, Lansbury made the case for a world economic conference. Roosevelt wanted to know what other governments would respond. Lansbury admitted that Baldwin would probably not be enthusiastic but thought he would respect a lead from the US. Would European countries welcome it? asked Roosevelt, adding, "You have not given me a peg to hang it on". George told him he would get the peg, that he (George) would visit the heads of state and rulers in Europe. While he was doing that, Dr Salter would raise public support by campaigning throughout Britain. President Roosevelt said that America would cooperate in arranging such a conference if Britain would join in taking the initiative.

No sooner was Lansbury back home than he visited Paris to talk to Léon Blum, the French Prime Minister and then continued with visits to leaders in Belgium, The Netherlands, Scandinavia, Czechoslovakia, Poland, Austria, Romania, Yugoslavia, Hungary and Bulgaria. He also had interviews with Hitler in Germany and Mussolini in Italy, who both politely welcomed his idea. But time had passed and he could not persuade the British Government to agree. It was urgently engaged in re-armament.

Disarmament

This has, of course, been a constant theme in LAP meetings and literature. The organisation owes its gratitude to Tony Benn for his cogent and stirring speeches and articles over many years, which have alerted readers and listeners to Britain's unhealthy nuclear relationship with the United States. The special relationship needs transformation by a declaration of independence from US weapons of mass destruction (WMD). Our hope lies in the eventual realisation that neither nuclear nor conventional weapons can defend Britain. Security does not come from the ability to create hell on earth, but from our ability to create a good and contributive society, the wellbeing of all its citizens and the environment in which we live.

The thought, passion and energy which Fenner Brockway and Philip Noel Baker, both in their 90s, brought to the setting up of the World Disarmament Campaign is what is needed to press a similar cause in the context of climate change. Today more than ever our priorities should not be military destruction but the protection of the world and its people.

Socialism

The story of one man whose remarkable life covered the emergence of socialism into mainstream British politics was the subject of Fenner Brockway's book *Socialism over Sixty Years* (1946).

The man was Fred Jowett, admired by the author for his integrity and focus on meeting human needs over and above his own career. Fred was a part-timer in a mill in Bradford, starting in the week of his eighth birthday, and became a full-timer at thirteen. He lived with his parents and four siblings in a one-up one-down back-to-back terraced house. No garden, but with a communal midden shared with neighbours, cleared out weekly at night by men with shovels. Work at the mill was hard and pay was low, a working day starting at 6.30 am and ending at 5.45 pm. Women worked up to a week before childbirth and returned to work a week afterwards. Mothers had to do this, since times were hard until the children were old enough to work.

A self-educated, avid reader, Fred found in socialism a way of lifting himself and his community also. Later, as a newly elected town councillor, he was described in the local paper: "A Labour chap! He looks (and sounds) like a good university student". Fred never moved away from his home town though, when he married, he found a decent modest house where he remained with his family. He died there in 1944 aged 82, with his latest article, newly published, in the paper beside him.

The Independent Labour Party (ILP) was to Fred and many others a part substitute for university, a forum where ideas could be shared, books discussed and political campaigns planned. Perhaps it was better than a university! [1]

Fred became an MP for a Bradford constituency and had a brief ministerial and cabinet appointment in Ramsey MacDonald's government until he lost his seat in the next election. The *Manchester Guardian* London correspondent wrote: "He is sure soon to be back at the House. Mr Jowett did many bold and useful things." MacDonald had given him the job of First Commissioner of Works (that is, steward of all government property). Five years of Tory Government were soon to follow and he found many other "bold and useful things" to do.

Out of office, the Labour Party needed inspiration and the ILP supplied it with a report, *Socialism in our Time: a Living Income.* This proposed that a future Labour government should establish a standard of life for all workers and start by setting a minimum wage and bringing in state allowances for children, the unemployed and sick and aged people. Other proposals were for a National Investment Board to direct the flow of capital and for banks to be socialised. Much derided by Ramsey MacDonald as well as the

---

[1] Keir Hardie had spoken of the need for workers to form their own party and many agreed. Groups sprang up around the country and the inaugural meeting of the ILP was held in January 1893, seven years before the Labour Party began. The press turned out in force to report on what some papers called the Impudent Little Party. It was impudent enough to continue until 1975, when it became a socialist publishing house.

Conservatives, *Socialism in our Time* had a great effect on socialist thinking all over the world, and still sets some unfinished agenda items for today.

Labour won the general election in 1929. This time MacDonald gave the "safe" post of Commissioner of Works to another genuine socialist who was immensely popular in the country - George Lansbury.

MacDonald opposed the *Living Income Report* with an explosion of wrath and bitterness, but he acknowledged that he had attacked it before he had read it, having seen the title *Socialism in our Time* over someone's shoulder in a train. He denounced the Independent Labour Party: "No parliamentary party worth its salt could allow its work to be settled for it by bodies that will not have to face the parliamentary attack."

Fred Jowett, ILP acting chairman, answered MacDonald on its behalf: "Our statement develops a series of coordinated proposals which we believe would lay the foundations of a new social order." It was, he said, the function of the Labour Party Conference, not the Parliamentary Party to decide the broad lines of policy. The ILP was within its rights in submitting them to the Labour Party. "If Mr MacDonald means that the approach to socialism must be decided by the parliamentary party... that would be an intolerable dictatorship."

It is tempting to speculate on what would have happened if the ILP had become the official Labour Party.

Will the demands placed upon us by climate change and the need for sustainability mean that our consumerist society will change, with scarce commodities and resources distributed as fairly as possible? If we care about the future we will need peace to focus on the demands of a changed situation, disarmament to stop wasting our resources, and socialism to share much better in a more equal society.

A system of rationing was well accepted during and after the Second World War: there was pleasure in knowing that the unequal distribution we had known was at an end, and that we had the means to survive.

As Gandhi put it: "The world has enough for our need, but not enough for our greed."

The more equal society that socialists have wanted for so long could make the difference between lapsing into the barbarism of the 'haves' defending their privileges at all costs and the 'have nots' resorting to desperate violence to obtain what they need. Socialism could avert that, if selfishness is put aside in favour of fairness and a spirit of human solidarity.

Endnotes

1. Gene Sharp, *Gandhi as a Political Strategist*, 1979, Porter Sargant Publishers, Inc., Boston, Mass. See p. 142.

2. Ibid. from Coretta Scott King's introduction.

3. Jonathan Schneer, *George Lansbury,* 1990, Manchester University Press, in the series *Lives of the Left*.

4. Fenner Brockway, *Bermondsey Story*, 1949, George Allen & Unwin. Brockway's *Socialism Over Sixty Years*, 1946, was also published by George Allen & Unwin.

CHAPTER ONE

POST WAR EUROPE AND THE H-BOMB

Early Years

At the Labour Peace Fellowship Annual General Meeting (AGM) in 1953 a new constitution was adopted. It declared itself "an association of members of the British Labour Party and its affiliated organisations." As its purposes and principles stated, it was "an organisation which united for joint action those members of the Labour Party and its affiliated organisations who (a) refuse individual participation in war and (b) those members who are willing to cooperate in non-violent methods for the promotion of peace". Its primary concerns can be summarised as follows:

- Working towards the ending of capitalism, fear and poverty, believing them to be the root causes of war. In a period of economic depression, capitalist economies relied on large scale re-armament programmes to stave off economic collapse and maintain full employment

- Highlighting the existence of vast military institutions as a menace to human brotherhood, which poisons the atmosphere for peaceful negotiation. It also called for an end to conscription

- Opposing imperialism, supporting colonial freedom and aid to under-developed countries, promoting the Labour Party's proposal for a World Plan for Mutual Aid

- Promoting the prime function of the United Nations as a peace-making body and supporting the work of the UN specialised agencies towards world unity.

Members of the Fellowship were expected to apply their principles to everyday affairs in local and national as well as international affairs, seeking to resolve disputes by peaceful means. These principles also should be applied within the Party "to promote a conciliatory spirit and tolerant attitude in all Party discussions."

In 1953 there were seven officers, ten National Council members and seventeen (non-executive) Vice Presidents. It could be thought that with so many people holding office there would have been a good supply of volunteers, but early newsletters constantly pleaded for people to come forward to share the work. As is still very often the case, LPF relied on one or two hard-working members to keep the organisation going.

The AGM deplored the decision of Bury Corporation to sack employees who were conscientious objectors and congratulated the local Labour Party and trade unions for their protest against this infringement of civil liberties by the Tory Council. It congratulated the National Association of Student Organisations which had come out in opposition to conscription.

The Treasurer reported a balance of £31. It was difficult to recruit members in isolated places and members of the local Hornsey Group stressed this was much easier if local groups could be established round the country. This policy was eventually adopted, after some opposition, the following year.

"Topic of the Month" in the May-June 1953 issue of *The Labour Peace Fellowship Bulletin*, written by Ron Huzzard, pointed out that progressive policies since 1945 had been seriously undermined by the crippling re-armament programme initiated following the start of the Korean War. It questioned whether the promises in the new Labour Party statement *Challenge to Britain,* setting out ambitious plans for social spending, could be kept. The arms bill, top priority, was now £5,200 million a year, and even the Tories had to spread it over five years instead of Labour's planned three. Britain should distance itself, he said, from the US and work towards the end of the Cold War.

German Re-armament and the H-Bomb

Early newsletters were duplicated and appeared bi-monthly for some years. The May-June 1954 issue advertised a delegate conference on German Re-armament organised by the London Co-operative Political Committee. Speakers were Sir Fred Messer MP and Ben Parkin MP. The fee was one shilling (10p).

A statement made to the Birmingham Conscientious Objectors Tribunal by one of LPF's younger members, Philip Mitchell, gave the socialist case against participation in war. His final words were: "I look for the day when the Labour Party will rediscover socialism and inspire the people of the world with a message of *peace through universal socialism*." As a conscientious objector, Philip Mitchell was sent to gaol for 6 months.

Victor Yates MP, in his Chairman's address to the 1954 AGM, asked how many Labour voters were socialists or knew the way to achieve real peace. The profit motive was the guiding hand in our economic system and lay behind the unrest in the colonies. As a result of the ending of British exploitation there, India was now a force for peace and was able to mediate between the US and the USSR. In the Labour Party, differences over the H-bomb had led 65 Labour MPs to support Frank Beswick's motion asking for parliamentary approval before Britain manufactured such weapons. Herbert Morrison had attacked Aneurin Bevan in the *Socialist Commentary* and the Party needed to resolve its differences on vital policy matters. Should we call for a ban on the H-bomb or should we support those who call for its manufacture in the hope that it will never be used? Yates added: "Pacifism is becoming more understood and we need to link it with socialist principles, both inside and outside the Labour Party".

The meeting was very exercised with the demand from the War Resisters International (WRI) that, if we wished to continue our affiliation now that we included non-pacifists in our membership, this should be on the basis of the number of LPF members who declared themselves "100% pacifist". It was left to the Secretary and the *Bulletin* Editor to negotiate with the WRI. There is no record of how the matter was resolved.

Reg Sorensen MP, in his last presidential address, referred to the danger of the H-bomb. "This growing rate of devastation may result in the annihilation of the earth". But the Ban the Bomb campaign was inadequate, as it only called for support for a petition already accepted by Parliament. Why call for the abolition of only one weapon? LPF should press for the successful outcome of the current talks to end the Cold War by the UN Disarmament Commission, oppose German and Japanese re-armament, support an end to colonialism, the establishment of a World Development Authority and increased economic and cultural contacts between East and West.

Later that summer, following a conference in Geneva on an Indo-China peace settlement, the LPF National Council passed the following resolution: *"The National Council of the Labour Peace Fellowship welcomes the truce in Indo-China. It believes it provides an example of the kind of peaceful negotiation that should be applied to resolving the outstanding issues of the 'cold war' in Europe as well as Asia. It therefore urges that the plans for rearming West Germany and incorporating her in the EDC (European Defence Community) be halted. It believes that Britain should press for further attempts by the Great Powers to reach agreement on German unity. It also believes that Britain should support the admission of the Peoples' Government of China into the United Nations and vote for this in UNO."*

In April 1954 Labour's Leader, Clement Attlee, gave a memorable speech on the implications of the H-bomb. His lead had been welcomed by all wings of the Party: right and left, pacifist and non-pacifist, Bevanite and anti-Bevanite. This could have been the start, said an article in the *Bulletin*, of a great peace campaign by the Labour Party. Instead, the right in the Parliamentary Labour Party and on the National Executive Committee chose to run a campaign in favour of German re-armament and the European Defence Community. This provoked widespread opposition in the Constituency Labour Parties (CLPs) and trade unions and served to deepen the division on foreign policy in the Labour Movement. It was particularly disappointing as Britain and France had acted independently from the US during the successful peace negotiations at the Geneva conference earlier that year.

1954 saw the first LPF public meeting at the Labour Party Annual Conference. Held in Scarborough, the topic was "Labour for Peace" and the speakers included the Reverend Donald Soper and Victor Yates.

The Fellowship was very encouraged by the number of resolutions on peace, colonialism and defence policies which had been submitted to Conference: 158 out of 433. 58 were against German re-armament, 54 were on atomic warfare, many calling for the banning of weapons of mass destruction. Others called for total opposition to any South East Asia military pact. There were 12 motions on military service, some calling for the end of conscription. On all these issues the National Executive Committee was criticised for failing to give the clear socialist lead that the rank and file had been calling for over many years. Many of the most critical motions came from the trade unions. Few would appear on the final Conference agenda as they would be composited (that is, merged with related motions): however, they gave a clear picture of the feelings of active Party members at that time.

Growing LPF influence

During the 1950s and 1960s, in the early days of television and before the internet, public meetings were frequent and well attended. The press - both local and national - reported speeches and debates in great detail. This was reflected in an account of a public meeting run by one of LPF's new local groups, in North London, in May 1954. Despite a pouring wet night, over 50 people heard Fenner Brockway MP and the writer James Avery Joyce speak on "Wage peace now – the answer to the H-bomb" and there were full accounts in three local papers. Members of the group had addressed eight local ward meetings in the previous few months.

By early 1955, LPF had grown and had a sounder financial base, so it was decided to launch a printed newsletter, *Labour Peace Leader*. Five issues were printed until funds again ran low two years later and the publication reverted to a duplicated format.

The European Defence Community

German re-armament continued to be a major concern in the mid-1950s and LPF spoke out against the Paris Agreements, which were the pre-cursor of NATO and dealt with the future of West Germany as a vital part of the European Defence Community. In Frankfurt in January 1955 a huge rally of socialists, trade unionists and church leaders, among others, rejected German re-armament, only ten years after the German military machine had wrought such suffering throughout the world. It sparked off widespread protests throughout West Germany. LPF condemned the failure of the British Labour Party and the French socialists to back this massive opposition by the West German people, despite Russia's offer to hold all-German elections. However, it welcomed the re-admission to the Parliamentary Labour Party of the six Labour MPs who had voted against the Paris Agreements.

Party discipline

The Party ruled with a rod of iron at this time. Ron Huzzard, newsletter editor, stood as a parliamentary candidate in Croydon North West in the 1955 general election. His election address included an uncompromising message against the H-Bomb and German re-armament and proclaimed his pacifist views. Sara Barker, the Party's National Agent, called him in, saying in no uncertain terms that the Party would not endorse him unless he watered down his statement. It was too late to replace him before polling day, and he decided, for the sake of the Party, to comply, but his message still made clear where he stood for peace.

Nineteen LPF members stood in the 1955 election, ten of whom were elected: Victor Yates (Ladywood), George Craddock (Bradford South), Frank Allaun (Salford East), Fenner Brockway (Eton and Slough), Emrys Hughes (Ayrshire South), Sir Fred Messer (Tottenham), Reg Sorensen (Leyton), Ernest Fernyhough (Jarrow), George Thomas (Cardiff West) and John Rankin (Govan).

Frank Allaun, who was to play such a big part in the LPF in the future, wrote his first article for the July 1955 *Leader*, focussing on the help the US had given to the Tories during the election campaign, reminding readers of the resolution passed at the historic 1952 Party

Conference which said: *"The cause of peace can best be served by sticking to our distinctive socialist principles and refusing to subordinate them to American, Russian or any other pressure".*

In his own election campaign, Frank found that the point most applauded at his meetings was that: "Britain – and particularly British Labour – should declare that it wants peace, friendship and trade with America and Russia but it will fight for neither."

India's leader Pandit Nehru was much admired for his independent peace policies and he suggested that Attlee could become the Nehru of the West.

Peace and international affairs were also on the agenda of many trade unions at that time, with resolutions to the 1955 TUC and Labour Party Conferences on the H-bomb, German re-armament and Apartheid in South Africa.

The Fellowship ran its most successful rally yet on the Monday evening of Party Conference, when 600 people heard Pastor Martin Niemöller and supporting speakers. He stressed the dangers of German re-armament, the West's call for a united Germany and the establishment of NATO. Victor Yates spoke of the LPF's opposition to the London and Paris Agreements, through which British troops would be stationed in Europe for 14 years. He and five other MPs had voted against this in Parliament. The Conference voted unanimously for a cut in the two-year call-up, as had the TUC that year. And the National Executive Committee (NEC) was becoming more left-wing. But it was disappointing, said Frank Allaun, in the December 1955 newsletter, that progressive resolutions were defeated by about $4^1/_2$ million to 3 million at the TUC and by $4^1/_2$ million to $1^1/_2$ million at the Labour Party Conference.

The National Council's main focus in early 1956 was to get the Labour Party and the TUC to implement their conference decisions on cutting the call-up. Letters had been exchanged with the Party's General Secretary.

The organisation was growing and had attracted a large donation from a major trade union and three Co-operative Women's Guilds. At its conference that Easter, the Co-operative Party opposed conscription, called for the total abolition of nuclear weapons and a cut in arms spending.

A number of LPF branches had been established and at this time there were branches in Reigate, Wimbledon, Thanet, Hull, Manchester and Ilford. The North London LPF branch was very active and had passed the following resolution in the spring of 1956:

"We are appalled at the disclosures by Mr Dulles that the USA has unilaterally used the threat of atom bombing on three recent occasions as a deliberate act of foreign policy. In view of the fact that the implementation of these threats would start a nuclear war in which Britain would automatically be involved we urge the closing down of American bases in this country and the withdrawal of Britain from all military alliances with the USA."

The February-March *Labour Peace Leader* published an article by GDH Cole: "Back to our Socialist Faith". He said: "The essential task for socialists today is to increase the number of really committed and active socialists who have a long-term ideal in their minds and who think and act in furtherance of this ideal and not merely in relation to immediate reforms. Socialism needs to make its appeal to men's deepest convictions and sentiments. Political parties cannot do this, as they have to win votes and appeal to doubtful or apathetic voters. If you are a committed socialist it is not these people you wish to concentrate on, but people who can be induced to put real energy into the Movement. If you can convince them, it is worthwhile."

He criticised modern parties for wasting too much energy on anti-Communism and not enough on positively promoting socialism. True socialism aimed for the abolition of class. Although the welfare state alleviated hardship and inequality, it did not diminish class and national barriers. He stressed the importance of disarmament and warned that while Britain continued to spend so much on arms it could not wage war on want.

Over the years the *Labour Peace Leader* and subsequent newsletters provided a snapshot of LPF thinking, its policies and activities. The May-June 1956 edition featured a decision taken at the AGM which reads:

"This AGM of the LPF welcomes the recent statements of the French Socialist Presidents M. Mollet and M. Pineau calling for an assessment of Western policy and the need to place disarmament as the first objective. We further welcome the election of the Socialist government in Ceylon. This Fellowship reaffirms its belief that socialists should be advocating an approach to international affairs that rejects reliance on armaments and alignment with either the US or Soviet power blocs. We urge the British Labour Party to adopt a new foreign policy that associates itself with India's stand for peace, reduces military expenditure and diverts resources to aid under-developed areas and works for a successful outcome to the UN discussions on world disarmament."

Cyprus, Suez and Oil

Fenner Brockway wrote in the October 1956 issue that the crises in both Suez and Cyprus were caused by economic imperialism. Britain clung to Cyprus to retain a military base to defend our oil interests in the Middle East and, for the same reason, the Tories wanted to keep control of the Suez Canal. He accurately predicted that:

"This is only the beginning. The next stage will be a conflict about the source of oil. America and Britain will soon have to face a demand for the nationalisation of the oil wells of Iraq, Saudi Arabia and Kuwait. At present there is a compromise between the US and British oil companies and the land-owning sheiks and kings. They share the swag fifty-fifty. But the Arabian peoples will not be content to exist in the most wretched poverty... and unrest grows."

"International socialism is the answer," he continued, "but we must not allow ourselves meanwhile to become the pawns of capitalism in Britain and America, which has no intention of surrendering its power to exploit. Self-determination for Cyprus, no war against Egypt, and support for the struggle of Arab people – these must be our resolutions in deeds as well as words."

The Suez crisis had resulted in an ignominious failure for Britain. At the LPF AGM in 1957 the Chairman, Victor Yates, said that it revealed the futility of violence. It was a tragedy, he said, that Labour had not opposed mobilisation from the start, but LPF had helped to persuade Labour to oppose the war when it started. The Tories had also had to reverse their policy over Cyprus, due to Labour pressure.

Mounting opposition to nuclear weapons

Well before the foundation of the Campaign for Nuclear Disarmament, Labour Pacifist Fellowship and the Labour movement as a whole were calling for the banning of nuclear weapons. The 1956 Labour Party Annual Conference had passed the following resolution:

"This Annual Labour Party Conference... declares itself opposed to the continuing of nuclear explosions and expresses its fear as to the dangers to humanity as a result of continuing radioactive contamination of the world's atmosphere and requires that the Labour Party should work towards the abolition of all nuclear weapons".

Recalling this decision, the 1957 LPF AGM passed an emergency resolution welcoming the decision of the Parliamentary Labour Party to call for a postponement of British H-bomb tests. The resolution urged the party to insist that Britain give a moral lead to break the disarmament deadlock by abandoning the manufacture and testing of thermo-nuclear weapons.

Britain had 1,000 atomic bombs, Russia had 10,000 and America had 32,500 – enough power to blow up the whole world. The Tories' 1957 Defence White Paper proposed a continuing huge arms bill. And German Chancellor Adenauer was calling for West Germany to have the bomb too. Members were reminded that, without reference to Parliament, the Labour Government had given bases in Britain to the US and spent £100 million on making the atomic bomb. LPF members were urged to promote the National Council for the Abolition of Nuclear Weapon Tests, which was founded by a Miss Fishwick, with support from Ron Huzzard and others.

At LPF's 1957 AGM delegates were appointed to the Central Board for Conscientious Objectors and the National Peace Council. Membership was increasing, the latest to join being Joyce Butler MP. There were now fifteen Labour MPs in membership. The annual fee was six shillings (30p) minimum. Finances were always strained and those members not going to the Party Conference were asked to send a postal order for 2/6^d (12p) towards the cost of the planned public meeting.

Resolutions to the 1957 Labour Party Annual Conference reflected the continuing concern of the rank and file about the direction of Britain's foreign policy: 127 out of 443 dealt with the H-bomb and disarmament, all calling for the ending of tests and a ban on atomic warfare. Many went further and called on the next Labour government to stop the manufacture of atomic weapons and dispose of existing stocks. Two went further still: Berwick and East Lothian asked for Britain to "investigate the technique of non-violent resistance" and Portsmouth South called for "the setting up of a National Commission to consider unarmed resistance as a national defence policy."

The LPF policy statement *Total Peace* (which sadly has no surviving copy) was produced for the previous year's Conference and seems to have helped to influence this thinking in the Labour movement. The trade unions too, were beginning to change. Frank Cousins of the Transport & General Workers Union (TGWU), was leading his union in a more progressive direction and its 1.25 million votes would make a big difference to Labour Party policy over the next few years.

But these signs of hope were at a time of continuing stalemate in disarmament talks. In the UK, the Tory government's 1957 Defence White Paper stated that over the last five years, defence expenditure had absorbed 10% of Britain's GDP - and 7% of the working population were in the Armed Services or supporting them. According to the August 1957 issue of *The Labour Peace Fellowship Bulletin*, these statistics were contrasted with growing world poverty. The average annual income in Britain was £300. In Tanganyika (now Tanzania) it was only £13.

Forward from War

This was the title of LPF's pamphlet published for the 1957 Annual Conference.   A big effort was made to publicise the LPF public meeting.   Leaflets were distributed through the Party's Head Office (inconceivable now!) and more were distributed, together with 500 pamphlets, to delegates and visitors.   In addition, 600 letters were sent to Constituency Labour Parties, seeking support for Portsmouth South CLP's resolution calling for a Royal Commission on non-violent defence. As a result, the LPF meeting was a great success.   And at Conference itself, Frank Allaun estimated that three-quarters of the CLPs had voted for the renunciation of nuclear weapons.

But what would a Labour Government actually do?   This was the Conference where Aneurin Bevan made his famous comment: "Without the bomb you would send a British Foreign Secretary naked into the conference chamber".   There was still a long way to go to translate Conference peace resolutions into a future Labour Government's foreign policy.

However, LPF MPs kept up the pressure in Parliament.   Following disturbing revelations in an answer to a Parliamentary question, Victor Yates and George Thomas put down an Early Day Motion protesting about American bombers with H-bombs on board, flying over Britain. This was supported within the first few days by 64 Labour MPs out of a total of 277.

Against a background of increasing tension between East and West, proposals for Neutral Zones in Central Europe were being taken more seriously. Austria was already such an area of disengagement, with agreement between the Soviet Union and the West. There were calls to extend this area to include East and West Germany, Poland, Hungary and Czechoslovakia.   And LPF urged Britain to follow the

Russians' lead in proposing a ban on arms deliveries to the Middle East by all the Great Powers.

The birth of the Campaign for Nuclear Disarmament (CND)

Following the inauguration of CND at a mass rally in London on 17 February 1958 and a huge demonstration in London, the first Easter March took place. Starting from Trafalgar Square it finished after some 55 miles at Aldermaston Atomic Weapons Establishment in Berkshire.

An early Aldermaston March

LPF was well represented and 19 Labour MPs had given the march their blessing. Several of them were in the lead with Harold Steele - the veteran peace campaigner, who the previous year had been to Japan, trying unsuccessfully to sail into the Christmas Island area, the site of atomic bomb tests.

Labour-TUC collaboration

A statement issued jointly by Labour and the Trade Union Congress at Labour's 1958 Local Government Conference listed the following aims:

1. Suspend British H-bomb tests
2. Stop H-bomb flights over Britain
3. No missile bases for the time being
4. A "peace zone" in Europe
5. World disarmament by stages.

These rather modest proposals were nevertheless a step forward. Much more radical was the resolution agreed at an LPF London conference in early 1958 of Labour Party, Co-operative Party and trade union delegates. It said:

"This conference, opposing the flying overhead of planes loaded with nuclear weapons and the establishment of rocket bases in Britain, and believing that the deadlock over disarmament can only be broken by deeds as well as words and by a bold deal by this country, urges:

1. *Immediate Summit Talks in an effort to resolve outstanding problems between East and West*

2. *Opposition by Britain to the manufacture, use and testing of all nuclear weapons*

3. *A substantial reduction of conventional armaments on a planned basis*

4. *A diversion of resources to strengthen Britain's economy and contribute on an expanding scale to waging war on poverty in under-developed countries.*

It calls upon Labour Party members to devote their energies to achieving these ends."

Germ warfare

During 1959 the LPF Bulletin reported on questions to Prime Minister Harold Macmillan in Parliament by Labour MPs about what was going on at Porton Down, germ warfare establishment. True to form, the reply was: "It is to help provide defence..." Dr Brock Chisholm, Head of the World Health Organisation, put it more accurately:

"All the horrible diseases that have afflicted man down the ages are available to the aggressor in a bacteriological war. If anyone is still not convinced that war and suicide are synonymous this should convince them."

This issue also prompted the proposal by the Direct Action Committee Against Nuclear War to abstain from voting for General Election candidates who refused to pledge opposition to nuclear weapons. This was on the basis that there was no difference between the parties. But no Tory constituency associations or MPs supported CND; no Tory MP was a pacifist; and Labour's modest proposals for disarmament were not supported by the Conservatives.

The fight for unilateralism

Unfortunately, there are no records of LPF activities from early 1959 until December 1967. Nevertheless, we know that LPF continued to campaign through the years, which saw successive key events: the start of the Vietnam War in 1959; the 1962 Cuban missile crisis; and at home the battle in the Labour Party for unilateral nuclear disarmament.

Labour Leader Hugh Gaitskell resisted attempts to commit Labour to unilateralism – losing the vote at the 1960 Annual Conference and then rousing his supporters to "fight, fight and fight again to save the party we love". The decision was reversed the following year, but it remained a divisive issue and he was challenged unsuccessfully for the leadership in 1960 and again in 1961. He died in 1963 and was succeeded by Harold Wilson, who led the Party to victory at the General Election in 1964, with a narrow 4 seat majority, ending 13 years of Tory rule. Labour's parliamentary ranks now contained several more LPF members and the Fellowship continued to gain influence in the party and the trade unions, with many CLPS, TU and party branches and Co-operative parties affiliating. In 1966 Labour increased its majority to a comfortable 96.

Vietnam and Britain's arms spending

We pick up the strands of LPF's history again in 1967, which saw Beatty Feder as Secretary and Frank Allaun as Chairman. Frank was elected to the National Executive Committee for the first time. He would eventually become Chair of the Labour Party in 1979.

By this time, the LPF newsletter was once again in printed form and it never again had to resort to a duplicated bulletin. LPF's Labour Party Conference rally was, as usual, packed out. Speakers included MPs Jim Dickens, Hugh Jenkins, Anne Kerr, Ian Mikardo and Stan Newens. LPF's new policy statement *Priority for Peace* by Ron Huzzard and Walter Wolfgang was widely distributed to delegates and visitors.

In 1967 both the Labour Party and the TUC annual conferences had carried resolutions urging the Government to dissociate itself from US policy in Vietnam. They promoted support for the majority of the

UN in calling for an end to the US bombing of North Vietnam, an end to the war and the unification of North and South Vietnam. Support for American policy had contributed to widespread disillusionment in Labour's rank and file. LPF sent copies of both the Labour and TUC resolutions to all CLPs, urging them to press the Government, Labour MPs and the National Executive Committee to ensure that Conference decisions became Government policy.

The continuing economic uncertainty was also contributing to Labour's unpopularity. LPF believed that the £2,200 million spent annually on defence was a major factor in Britain's continuing balance of payments crises and weakened our economy in relation to those of our industrial competitors.

LPF declared that the Government's proposed defence budget cut of £100 million was inadequate and called for a massive cut in military spending by:

- Cancelling the purchase of F111 aircraft from the US

- Not proceeding further with the Polaris nuclear submarine programme

- Not expanding our bases in the Persian Gulf and the Indian Ocean after the withdrawal from Cyprus

- Terminating all East of Suez bases and military involvement in West Germany well before the next General Election.

The high level of Britain's military spending was to become a continuing focus for LPF campaigning for many years.

Britain's nuclear weapons

The Polaris submarine was launched in Barrow-in-Furness in November 1967. LPF member Albert Booth, MP for Barrow, showed great courage by marching at the head of a CND protest through the streets of Barrow to the launch, in a town where most of his constituents owed their jobs to the building of Polaris and where his political future depended on their electoral support. This stand for his principles was a lesson to all peace campaigners and politicians.

East – West talks

Although LPF had been invited to visit the Soviet Union many years before, the first evidence of such a visit was when Fred Bacon represented LPF on a peace delegation of several like-minded UK groups to the USSR in 1967. An exchange of views on a wide range of subjects - Vietnam, China's entry into the UN, the Middle East, Germany and nuclear weapons. These revealed agreement on most – but not all – issues. Fred asked about the position of conscientious objectors in the Soviet Union, to be told: "No one (except students who are exempted anyway) ever objects to military conscription". This was probably not the whole picture.

Party Democracy, Pakistan, Northern Ireland and the Common Market

There was growing disquiet in the Party about the way Annual Conference decisions were being ignored by Labour's leaders. In 1969 Beatty Feder wrote, as LPF Secretary, to all affiliated CLPS and trade unions to remind them that the Party's General Secretary, Morgan Phillips, had stated in *The Constitution of the Labour Party*, a document published in 1960, that "Annual Conference does not instruct the Parliamentary Party. It does instruct the National Executive Committee... [yet] the Parliamentary Party could not for long remain at loggerheads with Annual Conference without

40

disrupting the Party."   Beatty went on to say that LPF was particularly concerned that the Government's support for US policy in Vietnam and arms sales to Nigeria during the Biafran war were completely at variance with Conference decisions and she urged CLPs to write to the Prime Minister, their own MP or parliamentary candidate and the Party's General Secretary. The lack of democracy in the Labour Party was a growing problem for Labour and to a large extent continues to this day.

CHAPTER TWO

LABOUR IN OPPOSITION AND IN POWER

Two years later in 1971, with Labour in opposition, the Labour Peace Fellowship (now with the new title of Labour Action for Peace) received a reply from the National Executive Committee to say that, in future, it would publish an annual report on how it had dealt with Conference decisions during the year.

Pakistan

The international situation was changing, with issues such as the civil war between West and East Pakistan now much in the news. East Bengal had suffered mass killings by the West Pakistan army. Millions had fled to India and those remaining in East Pakistan (soon to be called Bangladesh) faced starvation. LAP held a public meeting at Westminster and, in early June 1971, sent a deputation to the Pakistani High Commissioner to protest about military action and oppression.

The group was led by Frank Allaun and included Albert Booth MP, Robert Cross, Ron Huzzard and Walter Wolfgang. They were joined by MPs Peter Shore and Michael Barnes. On 15 June the LAP Executive Committee issued the following statement:

"Labour Action for Peace, appalled at the killing in East Pakistan, urges the British Government to use its full influence for peace by pressing for:
1. Immediate withdrawal of all West Pakistan troops from East Pakistan
2. The stopping of further aid to West Pakistan until troops are withdrawn

3. The admission into East Pakistan and the Indian border areas of UN relief workers and observers
4. The appointment of a UN mediator who will aim at securing the cessation of hostilities."

Northern Ireland

LAP's National Council issued a statement on Northern Ireland in April 1971, condemning the army's intimidation of the Catholic population, the house-to-house searches and use of CS gas (that is, tear gas, used for riot control). These tactics were exacerbating the situation. It called for political and economic policies such as the enactment of a Bill of Rights to outlaw religious discrimination, the provision of jobs and a crash programme of house building. It would take many years - and a Labour government - before the peace process bore fruit in Northern Ireland.

The Common Market

The economic arguments for and against Britain joining the Common Market were being well rehearsed during 1971, but as an article by Ron Huzzard in the July 1971 LAP newsletter pointed out, a little-discussed factor was the proposal for a common European defence policy, including a British-French nuclear weapon capability. Such developments would be supported by the US, as they would relieve pressure on the US to keep a military presence in Europe at a time when it was hard-pressed in Vietnam.   This reasoning meant many peace activists were anti-Common Market.

LAP lobbies the Government

The 1972 Annual Conference edition of the *Labour Peace Newsletter* called for the dissolution of NATO (created in 1949) and the Warsaw Pact (which was created in response five years later in 1953). Labour's new policy document *Programme for Britain* glossed over this, although it advocated a cut in the arms bill. This was currently 5.2% of Britain's Gross Domestic Product (GDP) - higher than any other European country except Portugal, which at the time was heavily involved in colonial wars.

By 1974, Labour was back in office, albeit as a minority government until another election in October of that year gave them a working majority. In May that year, LAP posed the question: "What is Britain's foreign policy now?" In fact, policy had hardly changed since Ernest Bevin was at the Foreign Office and Churchill made his "cold war" Fulton speech in 1946. Since then, our adherence to US foreign policy had been a priority for both Labour and Tory governments.

The crippling arms burden had led to welfare cuts and exacerbated Britain's balance of payments problems. US policy had led to CIA backing for right wing dictatorships in Greece and Portugal, Latin America and South Vietnam. Now Labour's policies seemed to be taking a new direction, with the election manifesto commitment to cut the UK arms bill to the average West European level. LAP set out further changes it believed were vital:

Unilateral action to abolish all nuclear weapons and bases in Britain; and the Vienna and Helsinki talks currently taking place to feature Labour's 1972 Conference decision to promote:

1. An all-European security conference to dissolve NATO and the Warsaw Pact

2. An increase in overseas aid, which could be achieved through arms cuts and the change in Common Market trading patterns

3. No arms sales to Chile, Greece, Portugal, South Africa or any of the world's flash points.

However, any hope that a new Labour government might change tack on arms spending was soon dashed. The July 1974 newsletter reported the increase in Britain's arms bill to £3,712 million. LAP had sent deputations to Foreign and Defence Ministers in May 1974. Harry Robertson (LAP Secretary) and Ron Huzzard met Foreign Office Minister Lord Goronwy Roberts, calling for Britain to urge the release of political prisoners in Greece and Indonesia; unilateral action on disarmament and arms sales; and for the Government to carry out the 1972 conference policy which called for the dissolution of the North Atlantic Treaty Organisation (NATO) and the Warsaw Pact.

A deputation to Roy Mason, Defence Minister (Terry Comerford, Harry Robertson, Ron Huzzard and Labour MPs Frank Allaun and Jo Richardson, together with Walter Wolfgang) pressed the moral case for disarmament. It called for these policies and also for Britain to opt out of a nuclear strategy, an end to US bases in Britain and for the abandonment of British plans to send warships to Chile. Although LAP was met with courtesy and attention it was left with the impression that the foreign and defence policies of the previous Tory Government would continue.

It was about this time that LAP produced a well-researched leaflet on arms cuts. It compared Britain's arms spending of £3,712 million with other NATO countries: Britain - 5.8% of GDP; France - 4.2%; West Germany - 4.0%; Italy - 3.1%. LAP countered the argument that cuts would mean unemployment. Arms cuts could increase the house building programme, lower income tax, fund increased pensions and provide grants for post-16 education.

Oil and the world economy

Speaking more presciently than perhaps he knew, Bob Edwards MP used a LAP public meeting in 1974 to highlight the grip the big oil companies had on the world economy and the potential threat this posed of future military conflict.

Broken manifesto promises

The next reference to a Labour Action for Peace pamphlet came in early 1975, when it was reported that NATSOPA (the print union) and LAP had ensured that every delegate to the 1974 Annual Conference had received a copy of *The Wasted £30,000,000* by Frank Allaun. This referred to the UK's current arms bill.

LAP called on its members to back the 54 Labour MPs who had voted against the Government's Defence Review in December 1974. Among these were Neil Kinnock and John Prescott, later to become Labour Leader and Deputy Leader. MPs writing articles in the February 1975 newsletter included Robin Cook on "More arms and more poverty", Jo Richardson on "NATO costs are crippling us", Frank Allaun on "Phoney arms cuts" and future MP Chris Mullin on "Diego García – menace to peace".

The Common Market

LAP continued to be concerned that the military and foreign policy aspects of joining the European Economic Community (EEC) were being ignored in the major debate taking place in the Labour movement in the run-up to the June 1975 referendum on whether or not Britain should join the Common Market. LAP had written to the NEC and the Government on this issue. It held a meeting in the House of Commons during the referendum campaign to hear both the pro- and anti-Common Market arguments. The Party was officially neutral, but the press was largely in favour and the 'Yes' campaign was much better financed and professionally run. The result was a foregone conclusion.

The Polaris nuclear weapon system

The February 1974 manifesto had promised that Labour would join multilateral negotiations for nuclear disarmament and seek the removal of American bases from Britain. Its October 1974 manifesto had pledged not to develop a new generation of nuclear weapons. Yet a year later, Defence Secretary Roy Mason was ambivalent about Britain using the US test site in Nevada for a new nuclear weapon test, obviously to update the Polaris warhead. And in answer to a question in Parliament from Bob Cryer MP, the Defence Secretary said that any decision on Polaris bases in Britain would depend on the outcome of the All-European Security and the Mutual Ballistic Forces Reduction conferences. LAP urged Constituency Labour Parties and trade unions to send resolutions in protest to the 1975 Annual Conference. LAP's 1975 Annual General Meeting was attended by several new supportive Labour MPs. Another hopeful sign was that the National Executive Committee, for the first time for many years, was fully behind conference decisions and prepared to stand up to a Labour Government. Labour Action for Peace itself was thriving. It had new international contacts and published its newsletter six times a year.

Labour's Arabian war

In spite of a manifesto commitment to support liberation struggles against colonial rule, British armed forces were actively engaged in Oman, to back the Sultan against the liberation movement in the country. In the spring of 1975 LAP member Stan Newens MP, speaking in the House of Commons, had called it "Britain's Vietnam" and 87 MPs had called on the government to reconsider backing the Sultan. LAP cited Britain's oil interests as the real reason behind this flouting of manifesto policy.

South Africa

In June 1975 the LAP Executive deplored the British veto in the Security Council, along with France and the US, of an arms embargo against South Africa. It called on the government to uphold its opposition to Apartheid and to support the struggle for independence by the African peoples.

Arms conversion

Faced with unemployment in the 1970s, workers at the Lucas Aerospace Company produced a "Corporate Plan" for converting the production of military aircraft and equipment to socially useful products and for people's needs to be put before the owners' profits. Nearly half the company's production was related to combat aircraft and the Sting Ray missile system for NATO. The company had been backed by the government, who wanted a strong and efficient aerospace company to compete with other European manufacturers.

But this meant rationalising the whole operation, by laying off 20% of the workforce and closing factories in Liverpool, Bradford and

Coventry. The various trade unions in Lucas Aerospace had come together and set up the Shop Stewards Combine Committee (SSCC) to create a single voice for all workers in any negotiations. This enabled the workforce to achieve much better pay and conditions.

Against this background, in 1976 the SSCC presented the alternative Corporate Plan to the management's proposals. It was based on considerable market research and detailed information on the machinery and equipment that all Lucas sites had, as well as the type of skills available within the company. The Plan proposed the production of high-tech medical, alternative energy and transportation equipment: production that was labour intensive as opposed to military production which was capital intensive, but highly profitable. Its aim was to head off job cuts by arguing that military production was neither the best use of resources nor in itself desirable. Lucas already had some expertise in the civilian field and sales, and no job losses would be needed.

However, it took three years before the management agreed to meet the shop stewards, and then only in a television studio, under popular pressure. They did not take kindly to the workers "telling them what to do" and rejected the Plan outright. Defence production continued, with rationalisation and job cuts.

The SSCC spent much time and energy lobbying the Labour Government, which - although paying lip service to the Plan - failed to act. The wider trade union movement, too, was unwilling to back the Plan, seeing its radical proposals as a threat to their established tradition of wage bargaining.

But many in the Labour Party, including Labour Action for Peace, championed the Plan. Bob Cryer MP, speaking in Parliament in February 1979, said: "The shop stewards' imaginative method of tackling the question of providing jobs for peace and not for destruction is an important moral crusade of which the House and the nation must take note." Although the Plan failed, it triggered successive campaigns for arms conversion and defence diversification which continue today.

Arms spending and the economy

In February 1976, in response to the balance of payments crisis, Chancellor Denis Healey wielded a brutal economy axe on public spending. But he spared prestigious military projects. Nuclear missile development, the Multi-Role Combat Aircraft (MRCA), new cruisers and Harrier jets went ahead, while crippling cuts were made in social welfare, education and other public services. The 1974 manifesto promise for real arms cuts and the 1975 annual conference policy decisions were swept aside. Arms spending was steadily rising.

Ian Mikardo MP, Chairman of the Labour Party International Committee and its Study Group on Arms Spending and Alternative Employment spoke at LAP's annual meeting in April, arguing the economic case for reduced arms spending to divert resources – money, manpower and materials – to manufacturing goods where there was consumer demand. He pointed out that the most prosperous countries spend less on arms.

Speaking in the Defence debate in the House of Commons on 1 April 1976, Robin Cook said: "It is spurious to distinguish between strategic and tactical nuclear weapons. The only reason why the super powers are able to call certain nuclear weapons tactical is that those weapons will not land in the heartlands of the super powers. They will come down on countries outside Russia and America. For Europeans, who are to have these tactical nuclear weapons dropped on them, the effect will be strategic, even if they are called tactical.

Many of these tactical weapons are of much greater explosive force than the bombs dropped on Japan in the Second World War.

"We are distressed when reading paragraph 27 of the Defence White Paper, that it is NATO's strategy: 'If deterrence fails to meet aggression with a defence tailored to the situation [this leaves us with the necessity of] selecting a suitable level of response from a wide range of options'. The language of that sentence is rather opaque but I hope we are not meant to take that as an endorsement of the Schlesinger doctrine of flexible nuclear options, which many of us find pernicious in that it is aimed to justify overkill capacity and can only bring nuclear war nearer by making it more easy to contemplate by giving it a credible strategy".

In response to Frank Allaun's amendment in the Defence Debate in January 1977, the highest ever number of Labour MPs (77) voted for real cuts in arms spending. Excluding Ministers, almost half the Parliamentary Labour Party voted to cut the colossal £6.1 billion per annum arms bill. LAP Chair, Frank Allaun, called on Labour's rank and file and the trade unions to back their demand. And LAP promptly took up the challenge, calling a public meeting in February in the House of Commons on "Welfare not Weapons". LAP also ran a large advert in April in *Labour Weekly* and *Tribune* backing the 77 Labour MPs.

Axe falls on aid

As well as cuts in welfare at home, overseas aid was axed. In spite of failing to meet the United Nations target of 0.7% GNP - and its own 1974 election manifesto target (*Public Expenditure White Paper, CMND 6393*) for aid spending, Britain's aid budget was only 0.38% (£448 million). It was now to be cut to £50 million each year for the next two years as part of the measures to satisfy the International Monetary Fund.

The Cold War hots up

In the 1977 June-July newsletter, Frank Allaun reported on Dr Frank Blackaby's letter to *The Guardian*, pointing out the illogicality behind the new US Defence Secretary's statement that, "as the consequence of the NATO decision to increase military spending by 16% over the next 5 years, the Warsaw Pact will be persuaded to stop increasing theirs". Blackaby also deplored Britain's involvement with the speeded-up plans to test an advanced H-bomb prototype in Nevada, expected to be the first of several. Aldermaston Atomic Weapons Research Establishment was working on two new all-British bombs, a miniature for the RAF and a new warhead for the Navy's Polaris submarines, along with the development of Cruise missiles to deliver these mini bombs.

Frank pointed out that the Labour Government, as well as the Labour Party, had pledged not to proceed with a new generation of nuclear weapons. He urged all those who opposed these developments to press the Government to resist NATO's demands for increased arms spending.

The MRCA Tornado

LAP was also highlighting a Granada TV *World in Action* programme, on the folly of plans to build the Multi-Role Combat Aircraft, known as the Tornado, which was being produced jointly by Britain, Italy and West Germany. It was described as being "too expensive, too complicated and too late" by military experts. Germany was responsible for the centre fuselage, while Britain was producing the front and rear. Italy was building the wings and yet another German company coordinated the various parts of the airframe and the hundreds of sub-contractors supplying other components. The project enabled Germany to participate in military production, from which it had been barred since 1945. By 1980, the cost was predicted to be £10 million. Pressure to get Britain into the Common Market was assumed to be behind this prestigious European project. The three countries involved saw different roles for the aircraft, only two of which were thought practicable by experts.

LAP Executive members had lobbied Dr David Owen, the Foreign Secretary, who assured them that the government took disarmament seriously. But the government had given in to NATO demands and pressure from the Tories. By 1978 arms costs had risen to over double the figure of four years previously. The arms bill would also rise by 3% per year for the next two years.

Against this background of soaring defence spending and cuts in welfare, Labour Action for Peace was growing, with more university Labour Clubs, trade unions and local Labour Party branches affiliating. At Annual Conference in 1978, Frank Allaun was elected Chairman of the Labour Party for the following 12 months - a crucial year when the election manifesto would be produced. Prior to the 1979 General Election, Labour Action for Peace sought a meeting with those drawing up the manifesto, as they had done before the 1974 election, when detailed disarmament proposals were promoted.

A significant decision by the 1978 Annual Conference for a commitment to nuclear disarmament was passed overwhelmingly on a show of hands and with the support of the National Executive Committee. It was expected therefore that this policy would feature in the manifesto. But this did not happen and, in any case, public disillusionment with the Labour Government and its economic policy was increasing and led inevitably to Labour losing the 1979 General Election, heralding the beginning of the Thatcherite era.

CHAPTER THREE

THE BEGINNING OF THE THATCHER ERA

Has Labour become the 'Peace Party'?

For a few years from the mid-1980s Ron Huzzard shared the editorship of the newsletter with a varied team of members, led by Michael Ormerod. From now on it was called *Labour Peace Action*, and was no longer printed as it had been for many years by Ripley Printers in Derbyshire. Now it was typeset and laid out by activists and printed in central London or Orpington. Gone was the somewhat dull and stolid appearance and there was a new, eye-catching masthead. Cartoons and graphics broke up the blocks of type, in the then current style of similar publications.

However the message remained the same - Labour needed to place peace "at the forefront of its policies". And now, in opposition, the Party moved to the Left, and became more receptive to LAP policies. Posters and leaflets were produced and LAP's call for a peace demonstration was taken up with a big peace march through London and a rally in Hyde Park organised by the Labour Party in June 1980. There were three unconditional demands:

- No Cruise missiles on British soil
- No new generation on nuclear weapons
- No increase in arms spending.

The rally, which was addressed by Michael Foot, shortly to become Labour's Leader, was preceded by a special party conference at Wembley following Labour's defeat in the General Election. Here Labour's policy, "Jobs, Peace and Freedom", was agreed by a five million vote majority. The next challenge was to ensure the Shadow

Cabinet campaigned for it. There was a growing awareness that party democracy had to be increased and constitutional changes had to be agreed by Annual Conference. Throughout the early 1980s battles between the old Right and the new Left led to big strides in making the leadership and the Parliamentary Labour Party more accountable to the rank and file. But it also led to problems with the Militant Tendency on the far Left and the breakaway of some of the Right to form the Social Democratic Party.

LAP fringe meeting, 1982 Labour Party Annual Conference. Left to right: Frank Allaun MP, Robin Cook MP, Joan Ruddick Helen John, Ron Todd (TGWU General Secretary) speaking. (RH)

Public reaction to Margaret Thatcher's Tory Government led to Labour gains at local government level. For the first time, innovative councils like the Greater London Council (GLC) under Ken Livingstone, Sheffield under David Blunkett and Islington under Margaret Hodge, set out radical policy changes, not only on ethnic minorities and women but on peace and nuclear policy.

Led by Manchester, many major local authorities became 'nuclear free zones' and the GLC ran a Year of Peace. Labour was also responding to the public mood which was increasingly apprehensive over the escalating tension between the Soviet Union and the US, with Britain endangered by the siting of Cruise missiles in the UK. The peace movement was flourishing as people flocked to peace meetings, marches, and rallies. Peace camps were set up at Greenham Common, Molesworth, Aldermaston, Menwith Hill and elsewhere.

In 1980 the Party's General Secretary was free to speak his mind in public. It seems inconceivable today, when the Party machine, ostensibly neutral on policy, in fact unfailingly supports the leadership. Ron Hayward, current General Secretary, was reported in *The Times* as speaking at length on the need for arms cuts and an end to poverty in the developing world: "The trade in arms is an obscenity and in the end can only lead to confrontation and conflict." He referred to the *Brandt Report*, which addressed international development issues and "Third World" poverty. The governments of the world now spent $540 billion each year on armaments. "Stand up for peace and do not be put off by the usual accusations of being 'reds under the beds'. We have suffered that taunt for 60 years, but it did not stop two world wars," he said. "Let us talk peace and declare war on poverty throughout the world."

The trade unions too were moving to the Left. The largest, the TGWU, under the leadership of Frank Cousins, was able to use its decisive voting powers to good effect on peace issues at successive Trade Union Congresses and Labour Party Conferences.

Frank Cousins Peace Award

This award was set up in 1984 to honour former TGWU General Secretary Frank Cousins' work for peace. It included a gold medal and a cash award to further research and promote the recipient's peace campaigning. It aimed to recognise the efforts of individuals and organisations for peace and disarmament. Labour Action for Peace members who have received the award include Fenner Brockway, Bruce Kent, Rae Street, Ron Huzzard, Frank Allaun, future Chair Beryl Huffinley and Labour Action for Peace itself.

One of the first references to the link between socialism and sustainability was the announcement, in the LAP newsletter of May 1980 of a meeting in the House of Commons organised by Labour Action for Peace. The topic was "Socialism and the Ecological Movement" and the speakers were Jo Richardson MP, Robin Cook MP and Stan Rosenthal of SERA (the Labour Environment Campaign).

The World Disarmament Campaign and international links

In 1979 Lords Fenner Brockway and Philip Noel Baker, with the support of LAP editor Ron Huzzard and Eric Messer, LAP Executive, had formed the World Disarmament Campaign (WDC) to further the aims of the 1978 UN Special Session on Disarmament. This became a worldwide campaign, and in the UK a petition committee was set up to gather signatures, to be presented to the 1982 UN Special Session on Disarmament. It succeeded in getting two and a quarter million signatures. Eric Messer was the secretary and other LAP members were active in the organisation. In April 1980, WDC held a huge

57

peace convention in Westminster Central Hall, attended by 2,500 people. It called for an end to the arms race and for resources to be diverted to alleviating world poverty. WDC never advocated unilateralism and some in the peace movement felt it did not go far enough, but because of its limited aims it had wider appeal.

At its Conference in 1980, the Labour Party went much further. It endorsed the call to divest nuclear arms unilaterally and resolved to remove all British and American nuclear bases from Britain. Michael Foot was elected Leader of the Parliamentary Labour Party (PLP) and Conference also agreed to widen the franchise for electing the Leader in the future. In response to a letter of congratulation from LAP Secretary, Cynthia Roberts, Foot sent a friendly and supportive letter to LAP.

It may seem surprising, but as long ago as 1980 the campaign against Trident began. Stan Newens MP, a LAP Vice Chair, sponsored an Early Day Motion opposing Trident as successor to Polaris. This was signed by 168 Labour MPs, a clear majority of the Parliamentary Labour Party.

In spite of being written off for its peace policies by the media, in August 1981 Labour was 16 points ahead in the opinion polls and had swept the board at the local elections in May. Public opposition to Cruise and Trident missiles was growing.

At the 1981 Party Conference in Brighton, LAP's increasing support enabled it to run a big rally in the Brighton Dome: "Human Race - Yes, Arms Race - No". Sponsors included CND, two Co-operative Political Committees, Brighton Co-operative Party and the Bertrand Russell Peace Foundation. Speakers were: Tony Benn, Prof Michael Pentz, Fenner Brockway, Philip Noel Baker, Alex Kitson, (Chairman of the

Labour Party), Bill Keys (SOGAT), and Joan Ruddock (Newbury Campaign Against the Missiles).

International links

Labour Action for Peace now began to develop international links, particularly with the Eastern bloc. Individual members visited places behind the Iron Curtain and LAP was represented by Rosalie Huzzard in a 19-strong peace delegation visiting the Soviet Union in January 1982, where they were guests of the Soviet Peace Committee. This followed the Peace Committee's visit to the UK in 1981 at the invitation of the Quaker Northern Friends Peace Board. Ron Huzzard represented Quaker Peace and Service Department. Fenner Brockway was also prominent on the delegation, which met government officials, academics, local peace committees, religious leaders and military personnel in Moscow, Leningrad, Tashkent and Samarkand. They exchanged views on peace education, arms conversion, conscientious objection, and the role of women, Poland, Afghanistan, international development, town twinning and the nuclear free zones. A Soviet army general suggested that a northern Europe nuclear free zone to include Britain and the Kola Peninsula would be a helpful move towards disarmament. At the final meeting Fenner Brockway presented a comprehensive Declaration for Peace, which included:

- The restoration of détente

- The urgent conclusion of the Geneva talks

- The prohibition of all first-strike weapons, nuclear weapon tests, the stockpiling of nuclear weapons and further development of weapons of mass destruction.

To everyone's delighted surprise, the Soviet Peace Committee agreed to co-sign this Declaration and the army general also added a further point: to strive for a UN declaration condemning nuclear war as a crime against humanity.

On his return, Fenner Brockway sought meetings with Labour Leader Michael Foot, Labour's National Executive Committee and the Prime Minister. LAP MPs were urged to raise the declaration in the House.

Women and Peace

After marching from Wales, the first "Greenham Women" set up camp outside the base at Greenham Common in Berkshire in September 1981. In spite of continual harassment, violence and vilification, they stayed there continuously for 19 years, until the missiles were withdrawn. Women everywhere were inspired by their witness in the face of such hardship and this led to a revival of the women's peace movement - demonstrating that women can bring a distinctive agenda to peace campaigning, based on non-hierarchical consensus, inclusivity and understanding of diversity. The spirit of Greenham lives on in the peace movement today. Many women in Labour Action for Peace were "Greenham Women" or supported the camp with visits and demonstrations.

LAP member Thalia Campbell raised funds to commission the statue "The Greenham Marcher" from the Maltese sculptor Anton Agius, commemorating the women's peace march from Wales to Greenham Common to set up the Women's Peace Camp. The statue (see next page) shows a woman holding in her left hand a bunch of brambles, nettles and thistles which the campaigners had presented to a US Commodore at the US base in Wellford. On her right arm she carries a baby who, in turn, is holding the dove of peace. The statue is now in Cardiff City Hall.

The Greenham Marcher, 2001. This postcard was produced and sold by the Women For Life On Earth (WFLOE) group.

The Falklands War

The war between Britain and Argentina started in April 1982, when Argentina invaded the Falkland Islands and South Georgia. War fever gripped the UK and boosted the fortunes of Margaret Thatcher, who saw herself as a great war leader in the mould of Winston Churchill.

Labour Peace Action exposed the hypocrisy of the Tory government's justification for the war:

- "We must not appease fascist dictatorships" - yet Britain had sold arms to Argentina and had also supported Pinochet in Chile.

- "The Falklands are British" - yet the previous year the Government had refused to grant full British citizenship to the Falklands inhabitants.

- "The islanders' wishes must be paramount" - yet all over the world Britain had ignored the wishes of indigenous people, for instance the forcible removal, against their wishes, (by a Labour Government) of the people of Diego García in 1966.

Instead, a negotiated settlement should have been sought. Sadly this was not a majority view in the Parliamentary Labour Party and, to LAP's bitter disappointment, the Labour Front Bench supported the war.

At Labour's 1982 conference too, there were signs that the fightback against Labour's peace policies had begun. Composite Resolution 51, expressing alarm over the arms race and re-affirming support for unilateral nuclear disarmament agreed at the 1980 and 1981 conferences, was passed by a 5:2 majority, decisive enough, according to party rules, for it to be included in the party's manifesto. But within 24 hours, Denis Healey and Roy Hattersley were on TV saying that these policies might not be in the manifesto. Reaction to this by the rank and file led to 70 Constituency Labour Parties along with trade unions flooding the next National Executive Committee meeting with opposing resolutions. But only 5 out of 17 members of the Shadow Cabinet supported peace policies and the NEC had a clear right wing majority. The NEC elections were also a disappointment. Left MPs Joan Maynard, Doug Hoyle and Eric Clarke were defeated by the trade union block vote and Frank Allaun, Judith Hart and Tony Benn were removed from positions of responsibility.

But Labour Action for Peace was determined to fight back. It organised a public meeting in the House of Commons, addressed by LAP member Jim Mortimer, then Labour's General Secretary, on "Implementing Labour's Peace Policies".

Arms Sales

Since its inception Labour Action for Peace had campaigned against arms sales. In the May-June 1983 newsletter, the editor reminded readers that Labour's 1982 Programme and a 1983 annual conference decision called for the abolition of the Defence Sales Office, the banning of arms sales to regressive regimes and to countries where the supply of arms would increase internal aggression. In 1983 Britain planned to sell £1,800 million of arms and military equipment. Recent Defence White Papers had revealed that profit from Britain's arms trade was helping to finance the cost of developing new weapons.

Talking Peace in the GDR

In January 1983, two LAP Executive members, Ron Huzzard and Gordon Schaffer, joined Norma Turner (Journalists Against Nuclear Extermination) and Terry Marsland (Tobacco Workers Union) on a delegation to East Germany (the German Democratic Republic) for talks on the critical situation between East and West in Europe. They met peace committees, trade unions and religious leaders. The East Germans felt that the US siting of Cruise and Pershing missiles in Europe increased the danger of nuclear war and they supported the USSR policy of arms reduction between East and West on an equal basis. They were also worried that German reunification would mean an end to the evolution of socialism.

Frank Allaun leaves Parliament

At LAP's 1983 AGM Frank Allaun, who had decided not to stand for re-election in Salford East at the general election, stood down as LAP Chair and was succeeded by Willie McElvey MP. A presentation was made to Frank for his contribution to Labour Action for Peace over many years, and he became LAP's first President.

Nuclear Free Zones

Until Thatcher clamped down on political action by local authorities at the ratepayers' expense, councils took advantage of their freedom to campaign for peace. By 1983, 150 local authorities had declared their intention to become 'nuclear free zones' (NFZ).

Labour-controlled Basildon District Council, for instance, planned a series of activities, in conjunction with the local CND groups, to publicise their declaration to become a nuclear free zone. These included: the planting of a Peace Tree; the erection of NFZ signs attached to road names on main roads entering the Council's boundaries; invitations to top speakers (including Fenner Brockway) to talk on peace issues; grant aid to the two local CND groups; a peace festival; a peace tableau in the town square to mark Hiroshima Day; articles on peace issues in the Council's newsletter, delivered to every household; a one-day peace school; erection of hoardings depicting a peace theme; showings of peace films; the preparation of peace packs for use in schools and adult education classes; posters and car stickers saying "Basildon - a Nuclear Free Zone"; and floral displays on peace in local parks.

Where now for LAP?

Labour Action for Peace had now become influential within Labour's rank and file. Membership was steadily increasing, policy papers were being distributed and public meetings were held throughout the year. LAP's fringe meetings at the Party's Annual Conference attracted huge audiences and LAP's newly designed badge was selling well. But a serious debate was taking place within the organisation.

Although the argument for "No Cruise, No Polaris, No Trident and No US bases on British soil" might have been won, the enormous difficulties of putting this into practice were recognised. How should Labour take the necessary steps to implement these policies? No matter how progressive Labour's Front Bench might be in opposition, in government it would be subject to enormous pressure from the military-industrial complex. The failure of the Wilson Government to stand up to these had been only too apparent. The way ahead must be more lobbying of Parliamentary spokespeople and the National Executive Committee, asking these difficult questions. In addition LAP's programme of meetings, newsletter circulation and press work must accelerate.

But the National Executive Committee's new document, *Defence and Security for Britain*, while maintaining a non-nuclear policy, retreated from cutting the arms bill - now the biggest of any European country. Under the Tories, the costs of the Falklands war and the development of the Trident nuclear weapon system were big factors. The next Labour Government would need to reverse the Tory cuts in welfare spending and to do this it would have to reduce defence expenditure. However, the NEC's document was agreed by a 5:1

majority at the 1984 Annual Conference and would form the basis of the next election manifesto. LAP supported it with reservations about its lack of clarity over arms spending and arms sales.

At the 1983 general election the question often posed on the doorstep was: "Won't Labour's policies leave Britain undefended?" Labour had not got the message across and the public were not clear about Labour's policies on defence. So in May 1985 Labour Action for Peace asked all its members and affiliated trade unions, CLPs and Labour Party branches to call on the NEC to run a nationwide campaign on its agreed peace policies, as they had done on the NHS, jobs and industry. LAP also circulated a model resolution for the 1985 Annual Conference calling for this initiative - and many CLPs and affiliates took this up. The affiliation of the Amalgamated Union of Engineering Workers (AUEW) and the General and Municipal Workers Union (GMB) to CND was also a hopeful sign.

Moscow Success

Another cause for hope was the mission to Moscow in the autumn of 1984 of the Labour Leader, Neil Kinnock and Deputy Leader, Denis Healey, to meet top Soviet officials. This showed it was possible to break out of the alarming spiral of the arms race. They reached an important agreement with President Chernenko, who made four commitments. The Soviet Union would:

- reduce and destroy the equivalent number of SS20 missiles when Labour scrapped Polaris

- make further reductions in SS20s for every Cruise missile launcher removed, provided it was not redeployed elsewhere in Europe

- take account of any decision to cancel Trident in the number of SS20s it deployed

- give an undertaking not to target nuclear warheads on Britain, if Britain removed all nuclear bases.

Chernenko also repeated the Soviet Union's commitment not to use nuclear weapons first in any military conflict.

LAP pointed out that Labour had done more for détente in one year than Thatcher had done in six. Her sour response to Labour's success in Moscow showed she was not interested in disarmament, unilateral or multilateral. Even US President Reagan had now accepted an offer of talks, leaving Britain in dangerous isolation as the only country bent on unilateral nuclear escalation. Talks to achieve mutual reductions in nuclear weapons could have given Britain real defence and released resources to aid economic recovery from the current recession.

Labour Action for Peace also continued to make international contacts. It sent delegations to Moscow, Peking (Beijing) and Sofia, at the invitation of the peace movements there. A group led by Willie McKelvey MP, LAP's Chair, also visited the GDR. Earlier in 1984 a group from the Soviet Committee for Cooperation and Peace were hosted in the UK by Labour Action for Peace.

In 1985 Ron Huzzard, now LAP Secretary, had visited China as a member of a delegation from the World Disarmament Campaign. China was making rapid strides in economic expansion and "capitalist investment to help socialist construction" was how the new economic measures were justified. As a small nuclear power, China intended to retain her nuclear stockpile until the superpowers disarmed, but she was playing a constructive role in the UN Conference on Disarmament. She had also announced a reduction in her armed forces of 1 million men over two years and a cut in real terms of arms expenditure from 17.5% to 12% of total government expenditure. LAP urged the British peace movement to widen its interest and contacts beyond the East-West confrontation and look as well to China and its growing influence.

LAP steps up its campaign

At Annual Conference in 1985, LAP ran its first stall in the conference centre, displaying newsletters, posters and other literature. Leaflets were handed out at various fringe meetings and delegates were given a statement by Gavin Strang MP before the debate on peace. LAP would continue to hold a stall at every conference, at first on its own, later jointly, with CND, the Campaign Against the Arms Trade (CAAT) or the World Disarmament Campaign.

Ron Huzzard and LAP member John Hamilton, Leader of Liverpool City Council (1983 - 1986), at LAP's stand at a Labour Party Annual Conference. (RH)

At the 1986 Annual Conference, LAP distributed 1,200 newsletters and sold many copies of its pamphlet. It ran two fringe meetings, in conjunction with Labour CND: one, attended by 120 people, on "End all US Bases" with speakers Tony Benn MP, Jo Richardson MP, Gavin Strang MP, Bill Morris (TGWU), Joan Ruddock (CND) and Peter Heathfield (NUM). The other, with an attendance of seventy, on "NATO and Labour's Policies", heard Tony Benn MP and Joan Maynard MP.

LAP's call for a Labour Party Peace Campaign was overwhelmingly supported by Conference. Other resolutions passed called for "No UK support for Star Wars" (US development and deployment of weapons in space), protested against arms sales and urged the promotion of arms conversion.

The newsletter was still produced regularly by Michael Ormerod, sometimes with help from others, and for every issue he managed to commission a number of articles by individual members, MPs and trade unionists.

Nuclear Weapon Tests

During 1985, LAP alerted Gavin Strang and the Labour Party to a service in Sweden monitoring underground nuclear tests. Those willing to make good use of this information could be notified quickly of any tests detected and LAP applied to receive this service. In reply to a Parliamentary Question from Gavin Strang, the Government claimed that no facility existed to detect tests of less than 5.5 kilotons of TNT, so a test ban treaty was not to be contemplated. However, most tests of strategic weapons were between 5 and 10 kilotons and, in May 1985, LAP published evidence contradicting the Government's assertion. This was confirmed in Geneva by the Swedish ambassador to the Conference on Disarmament. Sweden was confident that tests of no more than 1 kiloton could be monitored. The chief obstacle to a comprehensive test ban treaty was the unwillingness of the US and Britain to trust the USSR not to "cheat". The obstacle to progress was political, not technological. LAP reported that between March and July 1986 the Swedish service found that there had been three US tests in Nevada and two French tests in the Pacific. They varied in power from 4 to 150 kilotons.

Gorbachev's proposals for peace

Early in 1986, Soviet President Mikhail Gorbachev put forward a series of proposals to reduce the world's nuclear arsenal. They included the removal of Cruise, Pershing 2 and SS20 missiles from European soil. But US President Reagan turned down the proposals flat, and Margaret Thatcher, too, dismissed them outright. In fact, though constantly professing to support multilateral disarmament, the Tory Government had consistently turned down every move in this direction. It was opposed to a test ban treaty; it was opposed to a multilateral freeze on the development and deployment of nuclear weapons and the mutual scrapping of Cruise and SS20 missiles; and had not been present at any disarmament talks since coming to power in 1979.

The Labour Party and its leaders welcomed the Gorbachev proposals, seeking an immediate response from other NATO governments, as well as welcoming the Soviet moratorium on nuclear weapon tests.

Labour Action for Peace produced its next recorded pamphlet "Labour Arms and the Election", calling for a Labour Party Peace Campaign. It was written by Frank Allaun, Ron Huzzard and Michael Ormerod and had a foreword by Ron Todd, General Secretary of the TGWU. It was launched at Annual Conference in 1986. But the call for a big national campaign still went unheeded, in spite of its support from the Parliamentary Labour Party. LAP felt that, with 1986 designated by the UN as an International Year of Peace, the bilateral proposals for arms reduction presented to Kinnock and Healey in Moscow and the new Gorbachev proposals, the climate was ripe for real peace-making and international agreement - and the right time for Labour's peace campaign.

At last, following the overwhelming support for a campaign at Annual Conference, the pressure in which LAP had played a key role, bore fruit. The Labour Party head office asked all Constituency Labour Parties to appoint someone to coordinate at local level the Party's campaign on disarmament and defence, which was to start in December 1986. LAP urged members to pass on details of anyone appointed as Peace Coordinator for their CLP so that they could be kept in touch.

Chemical weapons threat

A new danger loomed however, as the US produced plans for the production of new chemical weapons, with the agreement of their NATO partners. The Geneva Protocol banned their use, but not their possession. Labour's Front Bench was totally opposed to the possession and deployment of chemical weapons, as was the Social Democratic Party (SPD) in West Germany, where they were in talks with the GDR to set up a chemical-weapons-free Central Europe. LAP called on Labour to hold urgent talks with the SPD to present a united front against the US proposals.

Who decides Labour's policy?

The Party's Peace Campaign pack contained much agreed policy:
- Cancel Trident
- Scrap Polaris
- Send Cruise missiles back
- Remove all US nuclear weapons from British soil
- A 'no first use' strategy within NATO.

71

It also dealt with other international issues: détente, the UN, South Africa, Nicaragua and overseas aid.

But LAP was concerned that the commitment to reduce military spending had been omitted - and that extra spending on conventional weapons was added. Who had authorised this change from policy supported by the National Executive Committee and agreed by Annual Conference in 1984?

A bigger blow to the peace movement came in July 1987, when Labour lost the General Election and the most jingoistic government of the post- war years was re-elected with a massive majority. LAP predicted that there would be tremendous pressure on the Party to scrap its hard-won policy on unilateral nuclear disarmament. So the reasons for adopting this policy needed to be spelt out and its gross distortion in the Tory media had to be countered. Thatcher's doctrine of self-interest above the public good had to be exposed.

Arms Conversion - the fight continues

The pioneering work of the Lucas Shop Stewards' Corporate Plan continued to inspire ongoing campaigning on arms conversion. In March 1987, the National Trade Union Defence Convention Committee held a conference in Manchester, which for the first time drew together many leading trade unionists working in the defence industries.

Also in March, the TGWU held a conference on arms conversion which was attended by 25 unions from 10 European countries, the first to bring together trade unionists engaged in defence industries in Europe. Everywhere defence workers were losing their jobs because of increasing Western dependence on nuclear weapons. Useful links made at the conference would continue through a European-wide forum.

Gorbachev's message to International Women's Conference

Marian Neville, an LAP Executive Committee member, was part of the UK delegation to the International Women's Democratic Federation Congress in Moscow in 1987, which was attended by 2,286 women from 154 countries.

Recognising the essential role that women could make in the process of peace building and conflict resolution, President Gorbachev addressed the Congress and, speaking with foresight, said that dwindling world resources in energy, along with hunger, disease and poverty in the developing world, were bound up with the task of eliminating the threat of nuclear war. There was no way to progress outside a non-nuclear non-violent world. Marian reported that there was unity among all the delegates that nothing can be attained without peace.

LAP at the UN

Another LAP Executive member, Noel Glynn, represented Labour Action for Peace at the UN Conference on Disarmament in August-September 1987. LAP's presentation was based on a resolution agreed at Labour's 1985 Annual Conference, which said that a future Labour Government must "work for a hunger-free world rather than trying to achieve world security through arms expenditure." Currently the UK overseas aid budget was less than half the UN minimum target, at only £1,200 million, while the UK arms bill was £18,500 million. A planned release of military resources was needed to combat world poverty. The UN needed to work to eliminate militarisation which was destabilising the economies and political systems in poorer countries. The ending of the arms trade and the burden of debt and protection of the environment were crucial.

What about the Russians?

Writing in the September 1987 newsletter, Tony Benn applauded the latest pamphlet *What about the Russians?*

"[This] is important because it goes below the surface of electoral rhetoric and looks at the world as it really is. It traces back the hostility to socialism in the Foreign Offices of the West to 1917 and reminds us all of the price the Soviet people have really paid in lives lost as the result of pre-war appeasement. ... Because it is a historical perspective with an analytical tone and a vision of the future, it should appeal to the majority of those who do not accept the way our present policies are being presented as the only alternative. For they are not, and the time has come when everyone in the Labour and trade union movement as well as the peace movement, must advance beyond the weapons debate to see how we can work for a new approach to the problems that face humanity."

In spite of a growing number of fringe meetings now held on LAP's traditional Monday evening, at the 1987 Annual Conference 120 people turned up to hear LAP's speakers at a packed meeting. Some were even turned away.

Cold War - the beginning of the end

By 1988 the first tentative signs of an end to the Cold War were appearing. Glasnost and Perestroika were beginning in the Soviet Union and peace talks in Washington had led to agreement in principle on the Intermediate-Range Nuclear Forces (INF) Treaty to ban land-based intermediate-range nuclear missiles. It was hoped that the US would ratify it, but Reagan, although faced with a huge budget deficit, had prevaricated, even on a 50% reduction in intercontinental weapons.

Labour Action for Peace submitted a paper to Labour's policy review *Britain in the World*, criticising Labour's performance in the last two elections in that it did not present its defence policies with conviction. The Party should re-think the Cold War mentality which had dominated Britain's (and Labour's) thinking since 1945. Labour needed to:

- Continue to oppose Trident

- Call for a ban on British nuclear testing

- Campaign against a switch by NATO to air-launched and submarine-launched missiles

- Adopt a policy of 'no first use' of nuclear weapons

- Drop its policy of increased conventional arms spending.

This call was backed by a pamphlet: *Warfare or Welfare: cutting the cost of militarism*. It was introduced by Ken Livingstone and was produced for the 1988 Annual Conference. LAP's fringe meeting there was on the same topic and was addressed by Bruce Kent, Tony Benn MP, Ron Todd (TGWU General Secretary), Jeremy Corbyn MP, Frank Allaun and Ron Huzzard. The pamphlet was recommended by Harry Cohen MP, LAP's Vice President, during the debate in Parliament on the Defence Estimates. It talked about how the cost, if war preparations had been consistently higher than our industrial competitors, could have plunged Britain into debt on our balance of payments. It argued that cutting back on defence expenditure and spending more on socially useful production could make Britain a safer place.

LAP argued that a non-nuclear policy need not be a vote loser. In Scotland, where Polaris was based at Holy Loch and the anti-nuclear movement was strong, Labour did well at the 1987 general election;

and support for the New Zealand Labour Party had rocketed, in spite of its nuclear-free policy.

More LAP international links

Margaret Glover and Noel Glynn represented LAP at the Third Special Session on Disarmament in New York in 1988 and submitted a statement on "The Social and Economic Cost of Militarisation". They reported a more hopeful atmosphere in the wake of the new superpowers' agreement. Margaret Glover went to a prior meeting in Geneva on Disarmament for Development and was heartened to learn that the USSR was already converting its arms industry to produce baby carriages, washing machines and fridges.

Rae Street, LAP's International Secretary, went to Georgia in the spring of 1988 and reported on the widespread resistance to the military-industrial complex. There was growing activity in the churches, the women's groups, the black communities, political groupings and organised labour. In the US too, she had found increasing awareness of the link between poverty and militarism. Everywhere there were signs of poverty reminiscent of the 1930s and of the inequality in American society. Time and again she was begged not to let the UK government break up the National Health Service. But of course, there were, and still are, completely different views held by the more affluent Americans.

In the April 1988 newsletter, Linda Clair gave an account of her visit to the West Bank and Gaza. She had been horrified by the brutality of Israeli soldiers who beat up families in the villages, imprisoned children as young as eight and destroyed food supplies. The inhuman treatment was only confirming the determination of the Palestinians to fight for justice.

Rae Street, LAP International Secretary (GCG)

In June 1988, Frank Allaun and Michael Ormerod represented LAP at a conference in East Berlin on Nuclear Free Zones. It was attended by over 1,000 delegates from 11 countries. Poland had been the first country to propose a NFZ in 1955 (the Rapacki Plan). Although this was rejected by NATO, a number of treaties prohibited the deployment of nuclear weapons in specific geographical areas: the Antarctic, outer space, the sea bed, Latin America and the South

Pacific. This last was proposed by the Australian Labour Party and the treaty was signed by 11 countries and ratified by all but two. Its terms were:

- The renouncing of nuclear weapons
- The prevention of the stationing and testing of such weapons in their territory
- Preventing the dumping of nuclear waste in their territory
- Ensuring that any export of nuclear material was for peaceful use.

Additional protocols (1) invited Britain, the US and France to apply the treaty's provisions in their own territories in the South Pacific and (2 and 3) invited the five nuclear weapon states not to use nuclear weapons against the other parties to the treaty - and not to carry out nuclear tests in the zones. Although China and the USSR agreed to 2 and 3, Britain, France and the US had not yet signed.

Fenner Brockway

Lord Fenner Brockway died in April 1988, just before his 100th birthday. He, more than anyone else, had been the main inspiration for the peace and labour movements for a generation. He had done much for Labour Action for Peace over the years and a tribute to his life by Ron Huzzard in the June 1988 newsletter concluded with the words: "We must continue the work for peace and socialism to which he devoted his life. He said 'LAP is the Labour Party group I am nearest to'. We will always remember his infectious optimism."

Labour abandons unilateralism and arms cuts

LAP now had a big task ahead. The defence section of Labour's policy review, published in 1989, was a bitter disappointment. The Party's agreed policy on both arms cuts and nuclear weapons had been reversed. And the Parliamentary Labour Party had abstained in the Defence Debate in Parliament instead of opposing the Tories' mounting arms bill. Only 30 MPs had stood firm.

There seemed little chance of reversing the position at Annual Conference. The rules had been changed to prevent delegates from moving amendments to the review and the leadership had sufficient support in the trade union section to ensure that it would be approved. However, the conference carried, by a two thirds majority, on a card vote Composite 47, a motion which reaffirmed Labour's earlier commitment to reduce arms spending to the level of other European countries and to transfer the savings made to the NHS, pensions, housing and other vital services; to investment in job creation; and to the restructuring of Britain's crumbling infrastructure. Under Clause V in the Party constitution, motions carried by such a majority had to be in the Party's programme and considered for inclusion in the election manifesto. LAP wrote to every Constituency Labour Party and affiliated trade union, asking them to urge Labour's leaders in Parliament and the NEC to support this policy.

"What about the Americans?"

The next LAP pamphlet posed questions about Labour's relations with the US, spelling out the extent of Britain's military involvement with the US; the huge number of US bases and weapons in the UK; the US attitude to Europe; and the position of peace and trade union movements in America. There were eight contributors, including MPs, MEPs, a former Trident missile engineer and a US peace activist.

A changed world

1989 was a turning point in the Cold War. The dramatic events in Eastern Europe - the collapse of communism and the break-up of the

Soviet Union - signalled profound changes in the balance of power worldwide. In Britain, although local Labour parties had not been invited to submit ideas to the latest round of the policy review process, Labour Action for Peace called on Labour's leaders to rethink the defence policy review of the previous year and to update it in the light of the these international developments.

However, the Defence and Security section of the 1990 policy document, *Looking to the Future,* went even further away from Labour's traditional policy. Earlier reviews said Labour looked forward to the time when tension between East and West meant that NATO and the Warsaw Pact could be simultaneously dissolved. Now it said that NATO would need to stay, in spite of the changes in the former Soviet bloc. NATO was, in fact, expanding its borders to the Oder-Neisse Line by absorbing East Germany. Gorbachev was calling for a new security system linked to the Commission on Security and Cooperation in Europe (CSCE) talks in Vienna. Such a system was provided for under Article 52 of the UN Charter. Why was Labour not supporting it? The retention of Trident, too, was running counter to the terms of the Non Proliferation Treaty. Arms cuts, agreed at the 1989 Annual Conference, were also not included in the document.

LAP's founder member speaks out

Writing in the March 1990 newsletter, Reverend Will Elliott, who was a co-founder of the Labour Pacifist Fellowship 50 years earlier, showed he was still politically forward-thinking. He urged disillusioned socialists not to join the Greens or other splinter parties, who were letting in the Tories by their electoral intervention. They should stay in the Labour Party and fight for socialism and peace.

New challenges

The United States was now increasingly dominant as the only world superpower. It was hoped that the collapse of communism would lead to a more stable situation internationally, with less reliance on vast military expenditure. Labour Action for Peace produced a pamphlet in 1990 entitled *Labour and Military Spending - Achieving the Peace Dividend*. It was introduced by Bill Morris, then TGWU Deputy General Secretary, with a postscript written by Bruce Kent. It focussed on the changes in Eastern Europe; on the loss of jobs in the defence industry; and on comparative arms spending by European countries. It stressed the need for Labour to reaffirm its policy to reduce arms costs and showed how to spend a peace dividend. With the Gulf War looming, a foreword spelt out LAP's opposition to the war and support for a peaceful solution based on economic pressure and diplomacy.

The Gulf War

This was sparked by Iraq's invasion of Kuwait in 1990. A UN-authorised coalition, led by the US, with Britain as its main ally, waged a fierce conflict in southern Iraq, setting oilfields on fire and deploying depleted uranium weapons, which caused cancer, deformed births and long-term illness in servicemen and Iraqi civilians. LAP members were prominent in the peace movement's campaign to end the war, with public meetings and rallies and a weekly march and demonstration in London, until the war ended in early 1991. But in an effort to get rid of Saddam Hussein the UN, under US influence, continued to target Iraq, imposing far-reaching sanctions which continued to affect the civilian population.

Campaigning against the Gulf War, 1991 (RH)

There was wide concern, not only over the war itself but also of the way the UN was used to sanction it. In 1991 LAP produced a pamphlet entitled *The UN - for war or peace?* In the foreword Bruce Kent argued that if there had not been such massive ignorance in the Labour Party about the UN Charter, there might have been more effective opposition to the war. Contributors included Tony Benn, Frank Blackaby (former director of the Stockholm International Peace Research Institute (SIPRI)), Ron Huzzard and Jim Mortimer, former Labour Party General Secretary. They argued that the Gulf War had led to questions about the need to reform the UN and suggested changes to make it more relevant to a new world order. The long-term aim should be to return to the principles laid down in the first Special Session on Disarmament (1978), in other words, the reduction of armaments by every state to the level needed for internal security and UN peacekeeping operations; and the control of the arms trade by the UN.

Labour retreats on disarmament

Labour's Annual Conference had voted for arms spending to be cut to the average European level in 1989, 1990 and now again in 1991, this time by a two-thirds majority on a card vote. Although this meant it was official party policy, Labour leader Neil Kinnock repudiated it.

The debate took place just after the US and the USSR had agreed mutual nuclear arms cuts - but this was not, alas, endorsed by Britain. The Party's Annual Conference rejected an anti-Trident motion, with the argument that possession of Trident was necessary in order to be at "the top table". This argument seemed to have won the day in spite of the fact that Britain had been excluded from the Strategic Arms Limitation Talks (SALT I, and SALT II) and the Strategic Arms Reduction Treaty (START) negotiations between the US and the USSR. But this was ignored. The Labour Party continued to change dramatically during the early 1990s. This made campaigning for peace within the Party even more difficult.

Although Labour was widely tipped to win the 1992 general election, the Tories retained power with a reduced majority of twenty-one. Witch-hunting by the National Executive Committee of those seen as on the Left, as well as disappointment with Labour's retreat on many of its policies, had lowered the morale of formerly active campaigners, and the general public, as always, turned away from a party they saw as divided.

As Neil Kinnock resigned after the general election, the subsequent leadership election saw LAP MPs Bernie Grant and Ken Livingstone contending - and focussing in their campaigns on arms cuts and other key international issues. John Smith now became Labour's new Leader.

LAP keeps up the pressure for peace

Labour had done better in the 1992 general election than in either of the previous two. The new Leader John Smith had respect for the membership. He spearheaded measures to end the trade union block vote and to introduce "one member one vote". In December 1992 he met a Labour Action for Peace delegation, something which had been denied to LAP for a number of years. The delegation included LAP President Frank Allaun, Ken Cameron (General Secretary, Fire Brigades Union (FBU)), Colin Christopher (Furniture Timber and Allied Trades Union (FTATU)) and LAP Secretary Ron Huzzard. A similar delegation had met the Shadow Defence Secretary, David Clark, in November. Both groups pressed for support in Parliament for arms cuts (as agreed by a 5:1 majority at Labour's 1992 conference, making it party policy); an end to nuclear weapons testing; support for a Comprehensive Test Ban Treaty and for an end to arms sales in the Middle East.

LAP circulated model resolutions on the peace dividend and Trident to all Constituency Labour Parties and trade unions. These were the two main issues in the defence debate at Annual Conference that year, with the resolution on arms cuts and arms conversion being passed by a 5:1 majority, thus becoming party policy. The fringe meeting filled the large Baronial Hall at Blackpool. LAP also held a fringe meeting at the Party's Euro Conference in 1992.

Publications included Frank Allaun's pamphlet *The Struggle for Peace - a personal account of 60 years' campaigning inside and outside Parliament*. It sold so well that it went to a third reprint. The newsletter continued to be published four times a year and LAP members wrote articles for the Left press, including the *Morning Star*, and had regular letters in the national press.

84

Arms conversion and no arms sales

In the House of Commons debate on Britain's Defence Industrial Base in May 1993, Labour's Shadow Defence Secretary David Clark said: "Since 1990, 100,000 workers in defence-related industries have lost their jobs. The Government have relied solely on market forces. ... Britain needs a diversification agency - a body that would ensure that defence companies were assisted with conversion work and diversified into other markets and products." Predictably the Tory Government rejected arms conversion as "absurd" and "left wing", but reluctantly supported diversification to tide the defence industry over temporarily during times of recession.

War in the Balkans

The newsletters of this period covered a wide range of issues: North Korea, illegal arms sales; the hijacking of the UN by the US: and the Balkans conflict. LAP supported the aims of "Peace in the Balkans", set up by LAP member Alice Mahon MP. Its aims were to support initiatives to promote lasting stabililty in the region, based on political and social not military solutions to the conflict.

A new Leader for Labour

John Smith's sudden death in May 1994 was a tragedy for the Party, and arguably for the country. At the time of his death, Labour was increasing its lead in the opinion polls and he could well have led Labour to win its massive majority in 1997 without the emasculation of the grassroots party organisation, the revision of Clause IV and the reliance on the markets that followed with the New Labour project.

In July, Labour Action for Peace addressed nine questions to the three contenders for the Labour leadership and deputy leadership: Margaret Beckett, Tony Blair and John Prescott. They included:

- Support for Labour's conference decisions (1989 - 1993) for arms spending to be reduced (in % GDP terms) to the average of other West European NATO countries

- Ending Britain's Trident nuclear weapons system

- Stopping activities in the Sellafield Thermal Oxide Reprocessing Plant (THORP) facility producing plutonium for export

- A big reduction in Britain's overseas arms sales

- A government defence diversification and conversion agency independent of the Ministry of Defence

- An all-European security organisation to replace NATO, based on the Organisation for Security and Cooperation and in Europe

- The reform of the United Nations

- Increased UK overseas aid to meet the UN target of 0.7% GNP

- Action by Britain to help cancel Third World debt.

CHAPTER FOUR

THE RISE OF NEW LABOUR

Profound changes in the Labour Party were to follow Tony Blair's accession to the Leadership. The amendments to Clause IV were just the start. The abolition of all but a carefully chosen few resolutions to Annual Conference meant it ceased to be a vehicle for ordinary party members and trade unionists to directly influence party policy. It became a mere rally, providing Shadow Cabinet MPs (and, when in power, Front Bench ministers) a platform to tell the wider public about their achievements.

Membership of the NEC and the National Policy Forum was manipulated from the centre by an often compliant staff and excluded anyone regarded as "Old Labour". Although Labour attracted many new members who saw the well-marketed New Labour project as relevant to their rising prosperity, many activists drifted away.

The New Labour Project

Under the new regime the Party continued to change. At the 1994 Annual Conference it was agreed that Labour should scrap Trident and link our defence spending to that of other European countries. But Conference also agreed another resolution, that the latter should only be "in the medium term" and the mover, the AEEU[2] General Secretary, finished by calling for more military aircraft orders. With two conflicting resolutions the Party ended up facing both ways. In

---

[2] AEEU was a merger between the Amalgamated Engineering Union and the Electrical, Electronic, Telecommunications and Plumbing Union.

the Commons defence debate in October, LAP member Llew Smith MP pointed out that the economic benefits of the peace dividend, agreed by Annual Conference the previous year, would now be lost along with the skills, talents and creativity that had been used in preparing for war. Why was Labour adopting this bipartisan approach when East-West tension had disappeared?

Labour's leaders simply ignored conference policy on Trident. The Shadow Defence Secretary, David Clark, dismissed the campaign against nuclear weapons as a "zany idea from the past". But, in the Defence Estimates debate in the House of Commons in October 1995, although the official Labour position was to abstain, 30 MPs voted against them. Alan Simpson MP quoted Field Marshal Lord Carver, who had said: "The trouble with nuclear arms is that we do not know what the bloody hell they are for. We cannot use them independently; we can't even run them without the help of the USA. Indeed no sane person would use them at all."

Conference too had changed. Gone were the boiler suits, the anoraks and the furious public rows with the platform of the 1980s. Sharp-shouldered black suits and briefcases, lobbyists and corporate exhibition stands were now predominant. The number of fringe meetings, often held by commercial firms, privatised industries and think tanks, serving canapés and wine, crowded out the left wing campaigners. Less time was spent in the conference hall and more was given over to "training schools" and "question and answer" sessions where Front Bench spokespeople told delegates how well Labour was doing. Annual Conference was managed as a media event, held behind massive security barriers.

Labour Action for Peace had to compete with a huge number of interest groups and usually held a fringe meeting, with a dwindling audience, with Labour CND. The LAP stand was shared with other groups and the last time LAP had its own stand was in 1997.

Such organisations as Labour Action for Peace were ignored by New Labour. The focus was on attracting the "middle ground", the place Labour needed to occupy if it was to win the next election. Every aspect of the Party's operation was geared to the right wing media, with a constant reminder to its public representatives that they had to be "on message". Sound bites for the headlines were constantly repeated. Blair's closing slogan at Conference in 1994 was: "Our Party - New Labour. Our mission - New Britain. New Labour - New Britain."

During his long parliamentary career, LAP activist Tam Dalyell MP always looked behind the official version of controversial events. He had always expressed doubts about the facts behind the sinking of the Belgrano during the Falklands War and the guilt of the alleged perpetrator of the Lockerbie crash. In April 1984, WPC Yvonne Fletcher was shot and killed outside the Libyan embassy in London during a protest against Gaddafi. Others were also injured. The shooting was followed by a siege of the embassy and the breakdown of diplomatic relations between Britain and Libya. After ten days, thirty Libyan diplomats were given diplomatic immunity and allowed to leave Britain. There was effectively no police investigation of Fletcher's murder.

Not everyone, including Tam Dalyell, was convinced that Libyans were to blame. In 1996 a Channel 4 *Dispatches* programme was shown, in which several respected crime and ballistic experts expressed doubts that the fatal shot could have come from the embassy. Following the programme, in a well-researched and measured speech *(Hansard 8 May 1996 Vol 277)* Dalyell raised the matter in Parliament. He pointed out that during the investigation the pathologist had changed his mind about the direction of the shot and there were other suspicious circumstances.

The Tory government spokesman dismissed the programme and Tam Dalyell's claims as "preposterous".

Stay in and fight

In October 1995 Labour Action for Peace gave a large 90th birthday party in the House of Commons for Gordon Schaffer, a longstanding member of its executive. Gordon had been a political and deputy editor of *Reynolds Sunday News*, later called *The Sunday Citizen*. He gave a spirited account of a lifetime of struggle for socialism and peace, and although he criticised some Labour leadership tendencies, he believed that Labour was the only mass party for the British working class. The decision to change Clause IV, taken at a special conference earlier that year, had led to much disillusionment on the Left and many had torn up their party cards in disgust.

Gordon Schaffer was not the only one to stay firm. At the 1996 LAP AGM Jim Mortimer urged members to show stamina, stay inside the Labour Party and fight for peace policies. He gave the example of Frank Cousins and Jack Jones in the 1950s and 1960s, who had stayed in the TGWU and fought for their beliefs when it was controlled by a right wing leadership. Now the union consistently advocated progressive policies. Jim pointed out that high military spending had undermined the Labour governments of 1950-51, 1964 -70 and 1974-79. Tony Benn urged party activists to fill the vacuum in Labour's thinking and relate LAP's peace policies to the needs of ordinary people. The Scottish Labour Party had taken this line when it ignored a plea by Tony Blair and, at its 1996 conference, called on a future Labour government to discontinue the Trident programme.

With the next general election approaching, LAP produced a statement which it sent to Robin Cook, Labour's Shadow Foreign Secretary (and a long standing LAP member) who was preparing a policy document for the 1996 Annual Conference. The LAP statement called on a future Labour Government to:

- honour Article VI of the Nuclear Non-Proliferation Treaty, under which all nuclear states, including Britain, should proceed to nuclear disarmament and general and complete disarmament

- oppose all nuclear weapon tests by Britain and others and actively promote the Comprehensive Test Ban Treaty

- respect any ruling by the World Court if it decides that any use or threatened use of nuclear weapons is illegal

- de-commission Trident as a step towards the goal of nuclear weapons abolition by the year 2000

- recognise that after the Chernobyl nuclear power plant disaster the links between nuclear weapons and nuclear power are now better understood and that a phasing out of nuclear power should be undertaken, with conversion plans for alternative forms of 'clean' energy

- faced with rising public spending and the demands of the Maastricht Treaty, reduce military spending to a level, in % GDP terms, no greater than other West European countries and spend the peace dividend, currently around £7.6 billion, on public services

- prior to the general election, establish a group of experts, including trade unionists, to draw up arms conversion and diversification plans to be quickly implemented by an incoming Labour government

- demand an end to the promotion of UK exports of weaponry and other military equipment to countries which violate human rights and pursue internal oppression and aggression to neighbouring states. It should wind down the Defence Export Services Organisation in the Ministry of Defence (MoD)

- in Ireland it should back the policies of its sister party, the Social Democratic and Labour Party (SDLP), its promotion of a United Ireland and its work in the Socialist International (SI)[3]

- propose that NATO should "wither away", as it has no credible role in the post-Cold War era.

The World Court Project

On 8 July 1996, only days after Labour's "Road to the Manifesto" had regrettably accepted Trident, the International Court of Justice (ICJ) gave a ruling on nuclear weapons. The World Court Project, which had Labour Action for Peace support, had asked for the ICJ's opinion on the legality of the use or threatened use of nuclear weapons. In a seminal legal opinion, the Court ruled that:

- Nuclear weapons (use or threat) are contrary to international law

- Nuclear arms defy the laws of humanity.

The Court felt unable to conclude whether or not the use of nuclear weapons could in extreme circumstances be judged as lawful, but the judgement gave a clear signal to the nuclear weapons states to proceed to disarmament which for Britain, would mean the end of all nuclear weapon tests and the decommissioning of Trident. LAP

---

[3] The worldwide organisation of social democratic, socialist and labour parties.

called on Labour's leaders to ensure that a new Labour government would take heed of the world's supreme legal authority.

At the Labour Party Annual Conference the following autumn, the motion on scrapping Trident was narrowly defeated. There had been huge pressure on delegates not to disagree with the leadership, so that the Party would appear united in the run up to the general election. Yet there was growing opposition to Trident from unlikely sources: Labour politicians on the traditional Right, General Lee Butler (former Commander-in-Chief, US Strategic Command) and a number of academics. But Labour's Front Bench spokespeople, using fallacious arguments about cost and keeping Britain's credential as a nuclear power "for a place at the 'top table" were determined to retain Trident.

Labour comes to power

Despite the changing nature of the party, LAP membership continued to grow and there were now 150 affiliated constituency and branch Labour Parties and trade unions. All LAP members were urged to work hard for Labour at the general election in May 1997. Labour won with a huge majority, ending eighteen years of Tory rule. Now 34 LAP members were MPs.

With Robin Cook as the new Foreign Secretary, there were welcome signs of a new international approach. The promise of an "ethical foreign policy", the banning of landmines, the proposed vetting of UK arms exports against the human rights record of the potential purchaser, were all welcomed. But why, LAP asked, was there no action at all on the most horrific violence of all: nuclear weapons - and Trident in particular? As Jeremy Corbyn MP said at a demonstration outside Downing Street in late May, "nuclear weapons are evil, immoral and unnecessary." An ethical foreign policy, he added, needs to be applied in relation to the development, deployment and use of nuclear weapons.

NATO expansion

With the inclusion of the Central and East European countries of the former Soviet bloc into NATO, there was widespread concern that its expansion to Russian borders could trigger a new cold war. The 1997 LAP AGM agreed the following resolution from Rae Street, LAP's International Secretary:

"This AGM of LAP notes that the Labour Party is committed to a 'nuclear weapon-free world' and to working for peace and security. We are therefore opposed:

- *to supporting a nuclear-armed NATO which has not abandoned the first use of nuclear weapons*

- *to the dangerous and de-stabilising policy of expanding NATO eastwards in Europe*

- *to further NATO arms procurement especially advanced technological weapons.*

We call on the Labour Party:

- *to support and press for greater resources for the Organisation for Security and Cooperation in Europe (OSCE) which was founded on the Helsinki principles which include conflict prevention and resolution by non-military means*

- *to support policies for disarmament in Europe and worldwide*

- *to support the formation of a European Nuclear Free Zone as a step towards a nuclear free world."*

A similar resolution was successfully moved by LAP European Commission member, Jim Addington, at the annual conference of the United Nations Association (UNA) later that spring.

LAP's pamphlet produced in 1997, *Say NO to NATO expansion: is the cold war coming back?* expanded this analysis. It was printed, as all LAP publications had been for many years, by Open Door Publications, based in North Wales (see Appendix II).

Diverting defence spending

The US estimated that 9,600 people were killed and 14,000 were wounded every year from uncleared mines. A massive mine clearance programme was needed to clear the estimated 80 million mines now in the ground. As international action was calling for a ban on landmines, Labour Action for Peace called on the Government to take the lead, with UN backing, to launch a programme of mine clearance, funded by an increasing proportion of the UK's defence budget. LAP suggested this should be included in the current Strategic Defence Review.

The Conservatives had let defence spending run away with itself. The Ministry of Defence was indicted by the National Audit Office in August for its overspend of £1.4 billion on its £10 billion procurement programme for weapons and military equipment. This overspend in one year was more than the extra funding for the National Health Service which Labour's Chancellor announced in his first budget.

An aggressive foreign policy

The Party's 1997 Annual Conference supported the retention of Trident by a small majority, similar to the results in 1995 and 1996. However, if UNISON (the public service trade union) had followed its own policy on the issue and not listened to the call from the Labour leadership, Conference would not have backed Trident retention.

The Party and the Government were now both out of step with public opinion. A Gallup poll, commissioned by the Nuclear Free Zone Authorities (many of whom were Labour controlled) was released during the conference. It found that:

- 59% believed that Britain would be more secure without nuclear weapons

- 63% disagreed with spending public money on Trident

- 87% wanted Britain to initiate the global elimination of nuclear arms.

117 MPs subsequently signed an Early Day Motion in support of the findings of this poll. It called on the government to respond by promoting policies leading to nuclear disarmament.

LAP was still active during the conference, with a much-visited stand and a well-attended meeting addressed by MPs Ann Clwyd, Tony Benn, Audrey Wise and Jeremy Corbyn, MEP Stan Newens and Ken Cameron (FBU General Secretary).

Eric Messer

Eric, who died in December, was a founder member of the Labour Pacifist Fellowship and continued to work for LAP until his death. Like his father, Sir Fred Messer MP, he worked in the Labour trade union and peace movements all his life. He helped found Victory for Socialism, which continued until the late 1960s to promote a Left agenda for the Labour Party. He served on Croydon Council for a while and was active in the Co-operative Party. He worked with

Fenner Brockway and Philip Noel Baker to found the World Disarmament Campaign.

Iraqi sanctions

In November LAP wrote to Foreign Secretary Robin Cook, welcoming the non-violent resolution of the current crisis in Iraq. However it deplored the UN's economic sanctions which, according to the UN Children's Fund (UNICEF), had caused the deaths of one million children and many adults. While condemning Saddam Hussein's obnoxious régime, LAP regretted the willingness of the UK government to go along with the US in threatening military action and pointed out that Iraq needed to be considered in the context of the wider Middle East, in particular the Israeli oppression of the Palestinians.

Responding to terrorism

The shape of things to come was foreseen in September 1998: LAP wrote to the Prime Minister expressing deep concern over the US threat to launch Cruise missiles without warning against Afghanistan and the Sudan - countries perceived as harbouring terrorists. Such moves, LAP said, would provoke, rather than prevent, terrorism; and it was possible that one day they would reciprocate by bombing raids on Western cities. LAP called on the Government to seek the immediate recall of the UN Security Council and to act as a conciliator rather than as partisan to US policy.

Northern Ireland

In late 1998 LAP Chair, Beryl Huffinley, wrote to Mo Mowlam, Minister for Northern Ireland, on behalf of the Executive, thanking her for her splendid efforts to secure the peace process in Northern Ireland. Mo wrote a very friendly letter in return, wishing LAP well.

LAP Chair, Beryl Huffinley (right) with Mo Mowlam MP,
Secretary of State for Northern Ireland (GCG)

During 1998 LAP Secretary Ron Huzzard was unwell and Michael Bechtloft became Acting Secretary. Ron died at the end of the year and LAP had to find its way without the political leadership and organising skills Ron had provided for 13 years as Secretary and as Editor and activist since LAP's foundation. A Memorial Meeting to pay tribute to Ron was held in the House of Commons in November 1999.

The bombing of Serbia

In the spring of 1999, for the first time, NATO's European states collectively attacked another European country. "The bombing of Serbia, without the approval of the UN, is an illegal act", said Jim

Addington, in an article in *Labour Peace Action Bulletin*. Yugoslavia and representatives of the Albanian majority living in Kosovo had agreed a new constitution for self-government, under which a joint group, including Serbia, could have policed the agreement. But NATO, unilaterally and in breach of the UN Charter, threatened the occupation of Kosovo. It initiated a severe and continuous bombing campaign to force a sovereign state to cede control over one of its provinces. The Russians voiced their anger over NATO's actions and the threat of a new cold war seemed a dangerous possibility.

In the early days of the bombing, LAP wrote to Foreign Secretary Robin Cook, Defence Secretary George Robertson, and Chancellor Gordon Brown, calling for the UK to pull out of the war.

Jim Addington, Action for UN Renewal and LAP Executive Committee, with Bruce Kent (right) (GCG)

Stop the War: UN not NATO

As NATO celebrated its 50th anniversary in April 1999, Jim Addington - active in Action for UN Renewal - wrote a critique on NATO in *Labour Peace Action Bulletin*. NATO had now become the leading player in the tragic wars in the former Yugoslavia. It was threatening to operate outside Europe and was increasingly abrogating to itself a military peacekeeping role "out of area", where the UN Security Council was unwilling to bomb recalcitrant states. Jim called for the people of the world, through their elected representatives, to work to reduce the power of the militarists and reassert the aim of the United Nations enshrined in its 1945 Charter, to "save succeeding generations from the scourge of war".

The newsletter announced a national march and rally in April against the bombing of Serbia and sanctions in Iraq. It quoted a statement about Iraq by Denis Halliday[4], former UN Assistant Secretary General: "Four to five thousand children are dying unnecessarily every month due to the impact of sanctions on Iraq. We are in the process of destroying an entire society ... It is illegal and immoral".

Tony Benn, speaking at LAP's AGM in March 2000 said: "Democracy is not what somebody will do for you if you just vote for them; democracy is what you do with your own life, controlling your own destiny by deciding where to put your own efforts. The Seattle outcry halted the World Trade Organisation (WTO) plan for corporations to take power away from nation states. This joint action by the many concerned organisations was a good end to the 20th century."

---

[4] Halliday resigned from his post as United Nations Humanitarian Coordinator in Iraq, and from the United Nations as a whole, effective 31 October 1998, after serving the organisation since mid-1964.

Tony argued that what was needed at this point was pressure on the Labour government to change its stance over Iraq and Kosovo. Without pressure from Labour's grassroots the government was giving way to the influence of the Murdoch press, the *Daily Mail* and the City of London. So many people felt left out, not listened to, while Labour's HQ was preoccupied with marketing and charisma. Clem Attlee had as much charisma as a mouse, yet Labour won the 1945 general election because the people wanted a change and Labour listened to and met their concerns.

Most people could not understand how Britain could spend billions on wars with Iraq and Kosovo but not provide helicopters to rescue those trapped by flooding. "War is part of the 'globalism' and saving lives isn't. Victims are not customers," Benn said. Big corporations like Walmart, Mitsubishi, General Motors and Ford were each bigger than many countries and were ruling the world.

9/11 and its consequences

There is a saying, "We all remember where we were when we heard the world-shattering news of..." Rosalie Huzzard recalls her experience of that fateful day in September 2001:

"A number of Left and peace groups such as LAP, Labour CND, the Women's International League for Peace and Freedom and the World Court Project came together to run a late night political cabaret, "Peace Exchange", during Annual Conferences in the early 2000s. On 11 September 2001, after demonstrating against the Arms Fair in Docklands, I joined the others at CND's national office in Holloway Road to plan that year's cabaret. During the meeting CND's media worker came up and said: 'A plane has flown into the World Trade Center in New York and another has attacked the Pentagon.' Then we heard that the second tower had been hit by another plane and thousands had been killed. Walter Wolfgang and I, still in shock, drove shakily to the LAP Executive Committee meeting in central London, pausing on the way in a neighbouring pub. Tony Benn, who had become LAP's President when Frank Allaun retired in 2000, joined us and we watched the full horror on TV. Tony said: 'The world will never be the same again. There will be war in Afghanistan'. How right he was."

Tony Benn 1993 (GCG)

This was the point when the "War on Terror" really started. The fear of Islam grew. Islamophobia gripped Britain and America and the situation across the Middle East steadily deteriorated. At Labour's Annual Conference two weeks later Tony Benn received a standing ovation when he spoke in the "Britain in the World" debate. He reminded delegates of the way in the past Labour had acted for peace. It had been the post-war Labour Government which signed the Charter of the United Nations. He cited three examples of Labour's leadership for peace:

- In 1950, when President Truman threatened to drop an atom bomb on Korea, Attlee flew to Washington and stopped it

- In 1956, when the Tory government said that we must fight Egypt's President Nasser, Gaitskell led the campaign against a Suez war

- Harold Wilson refused the US request to send troops to fight in Vietnam.

Now we must uphold the UN Charter. Any military action must be supported by the Security Council, not taken unilaterally. Tony reminded Conference of the preamble to the 1945 UN Charter, which says: "We, the peoples of the United Nations, determine to save succeeding generations from the scourge of war, which twice in our lifetime has caused untold sorrow to mankind". He concluded: "That was the pledge our generation gave to this generation and we have to renew it now".

Tony was to be awarded the Frank Cousins Peace Award in 2005, when he was presented with the gold medal at the TGWU Biennial Conference that summer. He paid a tribute to the union's great leaders, Frank Cousins and Ron Todd, saying that their socialism grew out of experience and so could not be shaken. He quoted Fenner Brockway, another great socialist who, as a young Liberal student, went to interview Keir Hardie. At the end of the interview Hardie said: "Put down your pen young man, I want to talk to you". When Fenner left the meeting, he was a socialist.

"No attack on Iraq"
Throughout 2002, as the build-up to the Iraq war continued, LAP worked with others to step up the campaign to try to prevent it. In March Alice Mahon MP, an LAP Vice President, tabled Early Day Motion 927 which expressed unease at the prospect that the Government might support United States military action against Iraq. It was signed by 133 MPs.

LAP Vice Chairs Alice Mahon MP and Tam Dalwell MP (GCG)

Writing in *Labour Peace Action Bulletin* in April, Jeremy Corbyn MP said that there had never been a time in LAP's long history when there had been a greater resonance to what it was saying within a deeply frustrated Labour Party and trade union movement. He deplored the Government action, taken without a debate in Parliament through the powers of the royal prerogative to send 1800 marines into Afghanistan to back up the bombing campaign and fight the Taliban and Al-Qaeda on the ground. The Labour Government was ignoring party members, the wider labour movement and public opinion in the country in its blind subservience to Bush and his US administration.

Jeremy Corbyn (GCG)

The situation in the Middle East prompted the birth of other anti-war groups such as Stop the War Coalition, Justice Not Vengeance, Active Resistance to the Roots of War and Voices in the Wilderness. Within the Labour movement the activities of Labour CND, which had been working for many years and the new organisation "Labour Against the War", meant that Labour Action for Peace was not the only voice for peace in the Labour Party.

The Iraq War

In August 2002 LAP Chair Beryl Huffinley wrote to the Prime Minister expressing LAP's opposition to any war with Iraq. LAP launched its latest pamphlet *Why War is not the Answer* during the Party Conference a month later. LAP's conference fringe meeting was shared with Labour CND and this partnership has continued for many years. The topic was "No War in Iraq, Reclaim the Party for Peace".

Labour Action for Peace was not only active against a war on Iraq. Missile defence, arms conversion, Trident and the Israeli-Palestinian conflict were all still campaigning issues. A mission statement was published in October 2002. It covered terrorism, nuclear arms, Iraq and the Middle East, the United Nations, a peace dividend and arms conversion and the arms trade (see Appendix I).

The Labour and peace movements, and LAP in particular, suffered a great blow when Frank Allaun died in November 2002. He had been a mainstay of the organisation for so many years, serving as Vice Chair and President, until he gave this up in 2001. LAP held a memorial meeting for Frank in the Jubilee Room in the House of Commons in March 2003, where tributes were paid to his unique and tireless commitment to the issues he held dear - housing at home and peace and disarmament abroad. As a one-time journalist he used his talents effectively in the press to further the causes he supported.

As the coming war on Iraq loomed ever closer, political activity intensified. LAP joined the growing protest in the lead up to the war, its MPs speaking out in Parliament and the Party's National Executive Committee, writing many letters to the Government. LAP members took part in the demonstrations held in Britain and worldwide on 15th February 2003. In London the protest, estimated at 1 million people, was the biggest in the capital's history. But it was to no avail and Britain joined the US in the invasion on 20 March.

Opposite: Getting ready to march against the Iraq War. From left to right, Rhona Badham, Grace Crookall-Greening and Rosalie Huzzard (GCG)

The chaos and violence which followed the invasion continued for years. Resolutions agreed at the 2004 AGM on a wide range of issues included: calling for an independent inquiry into the alleged torture by British forces of prisoners in Basra; condemning the illegal and immoral military attack on Iraq; and condemning US action in contravention of its obligations under the UN Charter.

LAP's International Secretary, Rae Street, reported on her visit to India to the World Social Forum. Here placards were everywhere, condemning US and British military action in Iraq. She contrasted the deep poverty and squalor in the streets of Mumbai with the $401 billion US spending on the military.

Throughout 2004 LAP continued to write to the Government and send out press releases on the deteriorating situation in Iraq and calling for the withdrawal of British troops by the end of the year.

CHAPTER FIVE

WHERE DO WE GO NOW?

Labour Action for Peace continued writing to the Government and the press to express its concern about the Iraq situation, where subsequent events proved that it (and the peace movement as a whole) had been right in their warnings of the breakdown of Iraqi society that would follow the invasion. The question of its legality and the aftermath are still with us today. The war undoubtedly had a profound effect on the Party, as members left in droves, hastening its decline. And even seven years later it was a contributory factor in Labour's defeat in the 2010 general election.

LAP still addressed other issues, passing resolutions at its June 2005 AGM on nuclear weapons; Palestine-Israel; and in support of the new Mayors for Peace declaration initiated by the Mayor of Hiroshima.

But there was concern about its decline as an organisation. Although existing members had been generous, fewer were renewing their membership as they left the Party because of the Labour Government's involvement in Iraq. Affiliations from local Labour Parties and trade unions were also fewer, as they were more attracted to Labour Against the War.

The 2005 AGM rejected a motion to wind up LAP and merge with Labour CND or Labour Against the War – because both those latter organisations restricted membership to Labour Party members, whereas LAP did not. Proposals were put forward to revitalise LAP's activities, with more regular newsletters, a new pamphlet, more support for the website manager Melvyn Harrison and closer association with Labour CND and Labour Against the War. LAP had a joint stand with the World Disarmament Campaign at the 2005

Annual Conference and joined Labour CND and CND very much as a junior partner in the fringe meeting on "Policies for Peace - no Trident replacement".

During the Defence debate at that year's conference, 82-year old veteran peace campaigner and longstanding LAP activist Walter Wolfgang shouted "Nonsense!" when the Foreign Secretary spoke about the reasons for invading Iraq. Hired "heavies" manhandled him out of the hall and out of the conference centre. He was refused re-entry, and deprived of his pass. The incident led to widespread fury at the tightly stage-managed event that Conference had become. Walter handled the huge press coverage brilliantly and the incident rebounded so badly on Labour's leadership that he was welcomed back by Blair the following day and received public apologies from the Prime Minister, the Foreign Secretary and almost everyone else in the Labour hierarchy.

But Walter described his treatment as trivial compared to the big "mistakes" of invading Iraq or holding nuclear weapons. "You cannot stifle debate by hiring heavies. A party has got to be open to the world. The Labour Party must get back to its culture of being open to argument. Let's hope this is a step on the way back," he said. Walter's reputation throughout the Party for his principled stand and handling of the media earned him a seat on the National Executive Committee, where he continued to fight effectively for peace and socialism until retirement two years later.

Since the 1940s, Labour Action for Peace has worked to keep peace and disarmament issues to the forefront of Labour's policy. It has sometimes been more effective than others, and has lasted longer than most pressure groups. The world is now more complex; politics and the mechanisms for change are less clear cut. There are hopeful signs such as the establishment of the International Criminal Court.

The ICC holds out the hope that the rule of law may one day take the place of war between nations, as it has within those nations which have been able to learn from their past internal conflicts. However, there is still work to do. The obscenity of Britain's huge military expenditure at a time when peoples' lives are being devastated by the Coalition Government's cuts in social spending need to be highlighted.

New methods of communication open up huge possibilities for speedy mobilisation and influence. In the wider world, socialists and peace campaigners need to focus on the threat to peace of the growing scarcity of natural resources and climate chaos, the continuing oppression and injustice in the Middle East and North Africa and the changing world order with the economic rise of India, China, Brazil and South Africa.

We hope the dedication and persistence of those of Labour Action for Peace - who worked so hard in the past - will inspire new, younger socialists to carry the work for peace and justice forward into a sustainable and peaceful future.

APPENDICES

Appendix I. Labour Action for Peace Mission Statement 2002

At this time of huge developments internationally and the threat of catastrophic war, Labour Action for Peace felt it was important to produce an overview of its position on all the major peace and disarmament issues of the day. The mission statement "Make Labour the Peace Party" states as follows:

Labour Action for Peace works inside the Labour Party to keep peace and disarmament issues to the forefront of Labour's policies.

TERRORISM: LAP believes that all-out war is no answer to terrorism. The only effective way to deal with such atrocities is by international action to bring the perpetrators before an independent world court and to end oppression and exploitation, the root causes of terrorism.

NUCLEAR ARMS: LAP continues to work for an end to nuclear weapons and bases in Britain and for a permanent end to nuclear testing. Trident must be cancelled, as decided at Labour's 1994 annual conference. Labour must work for the global elimination of nuclear weapons. LAP is totally opposed to the development by the US of a National Missile Defence programme. It calls upon the Government to reaffirm its commitment to the anti-Ballistic Missile Treaty that neither Fylingdales, Menwith Hill nor any other facilities in this country will be used for this development.

IRAQ AND THE MIDDLE EAST: LAP was opposed to the Gulf War in 1991 and has always opposed sanctions and continued bombing of Iraq. This could lead to catastrophe for the whole of the Middle East and increase the threat of terrorism in Britain and elsewhere in the West. The continuing Israeli/ Palestinian conflict can only be solved when Israel complies with UN resolutions, withdraws its settlements from the Occupied Territories and agrees to the creation of a Palestinian state with respected borders.

THE UNITED NATIONS: LAP believes that the United Nations should adhere to its Charter to 'save succeeding generations from the scourge of war'. It opposes the use of the UN to promote a US New World Order and believes that Britain should align itself with other European nations and the UN rather than being subservient to the US, whose expansionist policies in pursuit of its sown economic interests pose a growing threat to world peace. The UN should be reformed and strengthened.

LAP works for a diversion of resources from the global arms race to help the UN to be more effective in peacekeeping, disarmament, eliminating poverty in developing countries and tackling the environmental threats highlighted at UN conferences.

PEACE DIVIDEND AND ARMS CONVERSION; LAP presses for a continued decrease in arms spending and for the resources released to be diverted to social spending.

ARMS TRADE: Bearing in mind the need for an ethical foreign policy, LAP calls for an end to Britain's part in the bloody traffic in arms sales. It further calls upon the Government to stop Export Credit Guarantees being used for the export of arms and for the closure of the Defence Export Services Organisation, whose principal role is to promote arms sales.

This statement was sent to the Government and circulated widely.

Appendix II. Publications and press publicity

Throughout the years, LPF / LAP members regularly wrote letters to the press, both national and labour movement publications. Pamphlets were produced and from 1986 these appeared almost every year, and were launched at the Party's Annual Conference. They included:

Forward from War (1957)

The Wasted £30,000,000 (published jointly with NATSOPA) (1975).

Labour, Arms and the Election (1986).

What about the Russians? (1987).

Welfare or Warfare? (1988).

What about the Americans? (1989).

Labour and Military Spending - achieving the Peace Dividend (1990).

The Struggle for Peace (a short autobiography by Frank Allaun)(1991).

The UN - war or peace? (1991).

Arms Cuts, the Peace Dividend and Conversion (1993).

Reforming the UN! (1995).

Britain and the Bomb (1996).

Say No to NATO Expansion (1997).

Labour Peace Policy for the Millennium (1999)

US Domination - bad for Britain and the world (2000).

Ten ways for Britain to give a better lead (2001).

Why War is not the Answer (2002).

Frank Allaun - a Tribute (2003).

Future Security or Insecurity - which? (2004).

Appendix III. Officers and Executive Committee Members

Records are not complete but this is a snapshot of those who served Labour Action for Peace from its beginning:

1940
Founder members included: George Lansbury MP, Dr. Alfred Salter MP, Reg Sorensen MP, Rhys Davies MP, Councillor Richard West and Will Elliott.

1953
President: Reg Sorensen MP
Vice Presidents: Dr. A.D.Belden, Preston Benson, Fenner Brockway MP, Ritchie Calder, George Craddock MP, Lord Faringdon, Ernest Fernyhough MP, Emrys Hughes MP, Harold Lawrence, Sir Fred Messer MP, Minnie Pallister, Robert Pollard, John Rankin MP, Mabel Ridealgh, Dr. Donald Soper, George Thomas MP and Dame Sybil Thorndike.Joint Chairmen (sic): Audrey Jupp and Victor Yates MP.
Hon. Secretary: Denis Brian, Treasurer: Alderman Ted Simmons JP, Bulletin Editor: Ron Huzzard, Membership Secretary: Sam Edgeworth.National Council: Alderman Ted Berridge JP, Maurice Butcher, Norman Edwards, Will Elliott, James Avery Joyce, Ethel Watts, Councillor W. Martin, Elsie Pracy, Ron Smith, Richard West.

1957
Chairman: Victor Yates, Secretary: Terry Comerford, Treasurer: Allen Bullen, Editor: Ron Huzzard, Financial Secretary: Denis Brian.
National Council: MPs Frank Allaun, Reg Moss and George Craddock, also Ian Arnison, Maurice Butcher, L. Cumming, Elsie Pracy, Ethel Watts, W. Martin, Ron Keating, Michael Godfrey, Leslie Phillips, Richard West, Eva Ziegler, William Royle and J. Sandy.

1967
Chairman: Frank Allaun, Secretary: Beatty Feder, Treasurer: Arthur McDonough

1976

Chairman: Frank Allaun, Vice Chairmen: Lord Fenner Brockway, MPs Arthur Latham, John Mendelson, Renee Short, Jo Richardson, Stan Newens, Robin Cook and Jim Lamond. Secretary: Harry Robertson, Publications Editor: Ron Huzzard, Recruitment Officer: Ken Stevenson.

The Executive Committee included Walter Wolfgang, Eric Messer, George Wallis, Neils Toetcher, Michael Ormerod, Albert Tomlinson, Dan Smith and Frank McManus.

1978

Chairman, Frank Allaun, Vice Chairmen: Fenner Brockway, Robin Cook MP, Jim Lamond MP, Arthur Latham MP, Tom Litterick MP, Stan Newens MP, Jo Richardson MP and George Rodgers MP.Secretary: Harry Robertson. Treasurer: George Wallis, Publications Editor: Ron Huzzard, Secretary: Cynthia Roberts.

1983

Chairman: Willie McElvey MP, President: Frank Allaun.

1985

Chairman: Gavin Strang MP, Secretary: Ron Huzzard, Treasurer: Harry Robertson, Membership Secretary: Sue Kortlandt.

1989

Chairman: Brian Didsbury, Membership Secretary: Harry Robertson, Treasurer: Peter Wicks, Secretary Ron Huzzard.

1992

President: Frank Allaun, Chair: Brian Didsbury, Secretary: Ron Huzzard, Treasurer: Peter Wicks, Editor: Michael Ormerod, Membership Secretary: George Hutchinson, Vice Chairs: MPs Tony Benn, Jeremy Corbyn, Tam Dalyell and Audrey Wise. Others were Colin Christopher (FTATU), Bruce Kent, Jim Mortimer and Harry Robertson.

1997

President: Frank Allaun, Chair: Beryl Huffinley (following the death of Brian Didsbury), Secretary: Ron Huzzard, Treasurer: Peter Wicks, Membership Secretary: Melvin Harrison, Affiliations Secretary: Rosalie Huzzard, International Secretary: Rae Street.

1999

President: Frank Allaun, Chair: Beryl Huffinley, Secretary: Michael Bechtloft.

2000

Chair: Beryl Huffinley, Secretary and Acting Treasurer: Ron Barden, Editor: Grace Crookall-Greening,

2001

President: Tony Benn, Chair: Beryl Huffinley, Secretary: Malcolm Barker, Treasurer and Membership Secretary: Ron Barden, Editor: Grace Crookall-Greening.

2003

President: Tony Benn, Deputy President: Jeremy Corbyn, Chair: Beryl Huffinley, Vice Chair: Nicholas Russell, Secretary: Malcolm Barker, Treasurer and Membership Secretary: Ron Barden, Editor: Grace Crookall-Greening, Vice Presidents: included Tam Dalyell, Alice Mahon and Jim Mortimer.
Executive Committee: Jim Addington, Angela Bibb, George Goodfellow, George Hutchinson, Rosalie Huzzard, Walter Wolfgang.

2006

President: Tony Benn, Chair: Nicholas Russell, Secretary: Malcolm Barker, Treasurer and Membership Secretary: Ron Barden, Editor: Grace Crookall-Greening.

2007

President: Jeremy Corbyn, Vice Presidents: included Tony Benn and John McDonnell, Chair: Grace Crookall-Greening, Vice Chair: Nicholas Russell, Treasurer and Membership Secretary: Ron Barden, Joint Secretaries: Colin Bastin and Malcolm Barker.

2009

President: Jeremy Corbyn, Chair: Colin Bastin, Vice Chair and Editor: Grace Crookall-Greening, Secretary; Nicholas Russell, Treasurer and membership Secretary; Ron Barden.

2011

President: Jeremy Corbyn, Chair: Colin Bastin, Secretary: Richard Hart, Treasurer: Ron Barden.

Appendix IV. List of Abbreviations

ACAS	Advisory, Conciliation and Arbitration Service
AESD	Association of Engineering and Shipbuilding Draftsmen
AGM	Annual General Meeting
AUEW	Amalgamated Engineering and Electrical Union
CAAT	Campaign Against the Arms Trade
CND	Campaign for Nuclear Disarmament
CLP	Constituency Labour Party
CSCE	Commission on Security and Cooperation in Europe
EDC	European Defence Committee
FBU	Fire Brigades Union
FTATU	Furniture Timber and Allied Trades Union
GDP	Gross Domestic Product
GDR	German Democratic Republic
GLC	Greater London Council
GMB	General and Municipal Workers Union
GNP	Gross National Product
ICC	International Criminal Court
IFR	International Fellowship of Reconciliation
IJC	International Court of Justice
ILP	Independent Labour Party
INF	Intermediate-Range Nuclear Forces
LATW	Labour Against The War
LAP	Labour Action for Peace
LPF	Labour Pacifist Fellowship
MoD	Ministry of Defence
MRCA	Multi-Role Combat Aircraft
NATO	North Atlantic Treaty Organisation
NATSOPA	National Society of Operative Printers, Graphical and Media Personnel 1900-1987
NEC	National Executive Committee
NFZ	Nuclear Free Zone

NPC	National Peace Council
NUM	National Union of Mineworkers
OSCE	Organisation for Security and Cooperation in Europe
PLP	Parliamentary Labour Party
PPU	Peace Pledge Union
SALT	Strategic Arms Limitation Talks
SDLP	Social Democratic and Labour Party (Ireland)
SERA	Labour Environment Campaign
SI	Socialist International
SIPRI	Stockholm International Peace Research Institute
START	Strategic Arms Reduction Treaty
SOGAT	Society of Graphical and Allied Trades (the print industry union)
SSCC	Shop Stewards Combine Committee
TGWU	Transport and General Workers Union
THORP	Thermal Oxide Reprocessing Plant
TUC	Trades Union Congress
UDC	Union of Democratic Control
UNICEF	United Nations Children's Fund
UNISON	The public workers union
US	United States
USSR	Union of Soviet Socialist Republics
WDC	World Disarmament Campaign
WEA	Workers' Educational Association
WILPF	Women's International League for Peace and Freedom
WMD	Weapons of Mass Destruction
WRI	War Resisters International